Carl Royer, MA
Diana Royer, PhD

The Spectacle of Isolation in Horror Films
Dark Parades

Pre-publication
REVIEWS,
COMMENTARIES,
EVALUATIONS . . .

"**R**oyer and Royer deftly move from discussions of early landmark movies to present-day works while shifting with equal ease from canonical films such as *Freaks* to the more unexpected *Requiem for a Dream*. The result is a major contribution to literature on the horror film, a book that is new in every sense of the word. Highly recommended to both the specialist and the novice; both will have much to gain from its original insights."

Gary Rhodes
Assistant Professor,
Film/Video Studies,
University of Oklahoma;
Author, *Lugosi,
White Zombie: Anatomy
of a Horror Film,*
and *Horror at the Drive-In*

"**T**his book presents a finely-tuned study of horror cinema, covering an admirably wide range of films. It makes us think again about otherness and the popular imagination, turning to the details on the screen and bringing them back to life in a way that will make us want to see these films all over again. Horror is everywhere here: in cities, apartments, basements, bodies, space. It can be both grotesque and incandescent, terminal and redemptive. As they chronicle horror cinema's many features, the Royers draw out its wonderful capacity to speak to the human condition."

Ken Gelder
Reader in English,
University of Melbourne, Australia;
Author, *Reading the Vampire*
and *Popular Fiction: The Logics
and Practices of a Literary Field;*
Editor, *The Horror Reader*

The Haworth Press®
New York • London • Oxford

The Spectacle of Isolation in Horror Films
in Horror Films
Dark Parades

THE HAWORTH PRESS
Popular Culture
B. Lee Cooper, PhD
Senior Editor

Rock Music in American Popular Culture: Rock 'n' Roll Resources by B. Lee Cooper and Wayne S. Haney

Rock Music in American Popular Culture II: More Rock 'n' Roll Resources by B. Lee Cooper and Wayne S. Haney

Rock Music in American Popular Culture III: More Rock 'n' Roll Resources by B. Lee Cooper and Wayne S. Haney

Popular American Recording Pioneers: 1895-1925 by Tim Gracyk, with Frank Hoffmann

The Big Band Reader: Songs Favored by Swing Era Orchestras and Other Popular Ensembles by William E. Studwell and Mark Baldin

Circus Songs: An Annotated Anthology by William E. Studwell, Charles P. Conrad, and Bruce R. Schueneman

Great Awakenings: Popular Religion and Popular Culture by Marshall W. Fishwick

Popular Culture: Cavespace to Cyberspace by Marshall W. Fishwick

The Classic Rock and Roll Reader: Rock Music from Its Beginnings to the Mid-1970s by William E. Studwell and David F. Lonergan

Images of Elvis Presley in American Culture, 1977-1997: The Mystery Terrain by George Plasketes

The Americana Song Reader by William E. Studwell

The National and Religious Song Reader: Patriotic, Traditional, and Sacred Songs from Around the World by William E. Studwell

The Christmas Carol Reader by William E. Studwell

Popular Culture in a New Age by Marshall W. Fishwick

The Magic Window: American Television, 1939-1953 by James Von Schilling

The Spectacle of Isolation in Horror Films: Dark Parades by Carl Royer and Diana Royer

The Spectacle of Isolation in Horror Films
Dark Parades

Carl Royer, MA
Diana Royer, PhD

The Haworth Press®
New York • London • Oxford

For more information on this book or to order, visit
http://www.haworthpress.com/store/product.asp?sku=5347

or call 1-800-HAWORTH (800-429-6784) in the United States and Canada
or (607) 722-5857 outside the United States and Canada

or contact orders@HaworthPress.com

The Haworth Press, Inc., 10 Alice Street, Binghamton, NY 13904-1580.

Front cover painting by Carl Royer.

Cover design by Marylouise E. Doyle.

Library of Congress Cataloging-in-Publication Data

Royer, Carl.
   The spectacle of isolation in horror films : dark parades / Carl Royer, Diana Royer.
     p. cm.
   "Filmography."
   Includes bibliographical references.
   ISBN-13: 978-0-7890-2263-9 (hc. : alk. paper)
   ISBN-10: 0-7890-2263-X (hc. : alk. paper)
   ISBN-13: 978-0-7890-2264-6 (pbk. : alk. paper)
   ISBN-10: 0-7890-2264-8 (pbk. : alk. paper)
   1. Horror films— History and criticism. 2. Horror films—Psychological aspects. I. Royer, Diana, 1959- II. Title.

PN1995.9.H6R69 2005
791.43'6164—dc22
                                              2004020146

To Mary Lou Royer

and, as always, in memory of Carrie

ABOUT THE AUTHORS

Carl Royer, MA, is a writer living in Hamilton, Ohio. He received his BA in English from Temple University in Philadelphia and his MA in Creative Writing from Miami (Ohio) University. His short stories and poetry have appeared in various journals, including *Black Warrior Review, Ascent,* and *Allegheny Review,* and he has written for *Cairo Today.* He regularly presents papers on horror films at the annual Popular Culture Association (PCA) conferences.

Diana Royer, PhD, is Professor of English at Miami (Ohio) University, where she teaches courses in American and British literature and composition. She is the author of *A Critical Study of Nawal El Saadawi, Egyptian Writer and Activist,* and has co-edited volumes on American Indian cultures and regional writers. Her research interests also include death studies and horror films, subjects on which she has presented numerous conference papers.

CONTENTS

Foreword

Alone. Usually in a dark, unfamiliar place, somewhere at the border of civilization. Well, not quite alone. With you is someone or something that wants to kill you. This isolation is the essence of the horror genre. Characters in horror films confront the monsters in the border zone. Much the same can be said of horror filmmakers. They work within a genre outside of the comfortable mainstream, intentionally isolating themselves from popular taste (often perceived as "sick" or "demented" by genre skeptics) to dramatize in spectacular fashion the deepest fears of humankind. In this study, Diana and Carl Royer use the unifying theme of "spectacular isolation" to understand how horror cinema operates and, perhaps more important, *why* it speaks to us even as it disturbs us.

This is an ambitious task. Horror as a film genre traditionally defies easy definitions and neat categories. Perhaps this conceptual slippage is one reason why a growing number of academic studies of horror film have suffused the critical marketplace. These scholarly projects trot out their own theoretical agendas and corresponding close readings of examples taken from this most slippery of genres. Some horror cinema studies focus on general psychological approaches, such as Charles Derry's *Dark Dreams* (1977); the abject feminine body, Julia Kristeva's *Powers of Horror* (1980); philosophy and aesthetics, Noel Carroll's *The Philosophy of Horror* (1990); psychoanalytic interpretations, Barbara Creed's *The Monstrous-Feminine* (1993); body images, Linda Badley's *Film, Horror, and the Body Fantastic* (1995); Gothic horror, Judith Halberstam's *Skin Shows* (1995); gender, Carol Clover's *Men, Women, and Chain Saws* (1992) and editor Barry Keith Grant's collection *The Dread of Difference* (1996); and queer theory, Harry Benshoff's *Monsters in the Closet* (1997). Other studies zero in on specific variants or character types within the horror genre, such as Gregory Waller's *The Living and the Undead: From Bram Stoker's* Dracula *to Romero's* Dawn of the Dead (1986); Andrew Tudor's *Monsters and Mad Scientists* (1989); Vera Dika's *Games of Terror: Friday the 13th and the Films of the Stalker*

Cycle (1990); Andrea Weiss's *Vampires and Violets: Lesbians in the Cinema* (1992); Nina Auerbach's *Our Vampires, Ourselves* (1995); or my own *Psycho Paths: Tracking the Serial Killer Through Contemporary American Film and Fiction* (2000). Among the spate of academic studies of cinematic horror, this book is refreshing in its approach. As the authors state in their Preface, they are interested in creating a "more associative and imaginative approach to horror film studies than if we had been strictly theory-centric." The result is this free-ranging volume, which manages to pull off the enviable feat of being accessible and academic at the same time. As the title indicates, the Royers include a "dark parade" of films in this book, providing a variety one would normally associate with a collection of essays written by multiple authors. The Royers then exhibit enough intellectual confidence to let the works dictate the organization and scope of the various chapters, rather than forcing the films into a proscribed theoretical framework. Nevertheless, there is a thread that unites all of the disparate chapters—the idea of isolation as a crucial component of the horror genre.

Chapter 1, "Body Doubles and Severed Hands," explores the kinship between avant-garde film and exploitation/horror cinema, surely two genres on the margin of the mainstream but often perceived as aesthetically opposite (avant-garde as "high" culture, horror as "low"). Here, the Royers parallel Joan Hawkins in her study *Cutting Edge: Art-Horror and the Horrific Avant-Garde* (2000), in which Hawkins challenges the traditional binary opposition between the "high" culture of art cinema and "low" culture of horror film. As the chapter title indicates, the shocking "splatter" element associated with later horror film is anticipated by early experimental avant-garde filmmakers. The Royers wisely acknowledge the critical difficulty in classifying certain early films and directors as dadaist, surrealist, impressionist, et cetera, but they do point out there is little debate as to the surrealist status of Luis Buñuel's two films, *Un Chien Andalou* (1929) and *L'Âge d'or* (1930). The former, with its infamous image of the woman's eye sliced open by a razor, and the latter, with its fetishistic images that pathologize a couple's continuously frustrated sexual desire, clearly share many elements in common with horror cinema's graphic focus on body shocks and distorted sexuality. The Royers connect these two surrealist films with Tod Browning's exploitation film *Freaks* (1932), whose casting of real freak-show performers in a fictional freak show is, to say the least, surreal. Once this bridge has been constructed from the avant-garde to low-budget horror, the Royers gleefully collapse as many of the boundaries between art and exploitation as possible, examining works ranging from Alfred Hitchcock's *Psycho* (1960) to Darren Aronofsky's *Pi* (1998) and *Requiem for a Dream* (2000). Also mentioned are "fringe" but nevertheless important filmmakers such as John Waters and David Lynch. The overall benefit of this crossfertilization between avant-garde and horror cinema, according to the Royers, is that innovation and perhaps even art sometimes finds its way from the generic isolation of horror into mainstream formulaic cinema.

Chapter 2 centers on one of the most well-known of the auteurs to bring art into mainstream horror: Alfred Hitchcock. The Royers maintain that although Hitchcock is commonly labeled "the master of suspense," a more accurate title for him, given his narrative focus on taboo and/or sadomasochistic subjects, is "the master of horror." Of course, many people would agree that Hitchcock's serial-killer movie *Psycho* or his nature-strikes-back fantasy *The Birds* (1963) are situated within the horror genre; however, the Royers make the case that many of Hitchcock's suspense thrillers (such as *Sabotage* [1936], *Spellbound* [1945], *Strangers on a Train* [1951], and *Marnie* [1964]) contain enough horrific sequences and taboo violations at pivotal moments to nudge these films over into horror. Genre critics often note the doubling of characters and deliberate invocation of phobias in horror cinema, both of which are conspicuous elements of Hitchcock films. In fact, the use of the suspense format may have been an act of subterfuge on Hitchcock's part—a necessary deception foisted upon studio executives, censors, and indeed most of the filmgoing public— in order to explore otherwise "unspeakable" areas of the psyche. Through symbolism and sly suggestion, Hitchcock integrates into his work all manner of twisted sexuality, running the gamut from voyeurism to fetishism to sexual abuse to incest. Ironically enough, the Royers conclude of Hitchcock, his bringing of nightmares to mainstream audiences enables those same audiences to, as the authors put it so eloquently, "live with the nightmares we cannot avoid."

Chapter 3, "Horror, Humor, Poetry: Sam Raimi's *Evil Dead* Trilogy," examines the work of another auteur more directly associated with the horror genre. Although Sam Raimi has made the crossover into mainstream A-list directorial status with the megahit *Spider-*

Man (2002), he initially secured a place for himself in low-budget horror history with *The Evil Dead* (1981), *The Evil Dead II* (1987), and *Army of Darkness* (1993). These films are known for their explicit gore and slapstick humor (a quality especially evident in the two sequels to *The Evil Dead*). Yet these films, the Royers contend, "always contain extended passages of poetic beauty." Much like Hitchcock, Raimi infuses all of his work, from the early horror to the later mainstream, with a certain visual lyricism and thematic unity. The campy "splatter" of the *Evil Dead* movies may disguise Raimi's complex shifting of point of view, kinetic camera movement, surprisingly subtle foreshadowing of future mayhem, and satirical sensibility, but all of these qualities are present, as the Royers demonstrate. These are qualities that Raimi is bringing over into his mainstream work, having learned them so well in the isolated border zone of horror.

Another auteur who infuses elements of horror into his films is Canadian-born David Cronenberg, whose work is the subject of Chapter 4. Cronenberg, fascinated with the theme of human evolution and development in societies that are de-evolving, creates films that, perhaps surprisingly for a director who is an avowed atheist, present the martyrdom of main characters in their quests for spiritually redemptive growth and connection with others in nihilistic worlds. Thus, while the films conclude that isolation is the norm for human existence, there remains within each individual the need for merging with other identities. One of the more literary filmmakers, Cronenberg consistently presents the archetypal "mad scientist" character as a messianic figure whose fate, while tragic and usually bloody, is an outgrowth of an obsessive metaphysical drive for unification with other isolated individuals. This merging of selves, given Cronenberg's inclination toward horror, is as physically destructive as it is spectacular, but it is still ultimately redemptive. The Royers, refreshingly against the critical grain, make the compelling case that Cronenberg's vision, although bleak, is more optimistic than pessimistic in films such as *Videodrome* (1983), *The Fly* (1986), *Crash* (1996), and *eXistenZ* (1999).

In Chapter 5, the Royers shift their focus from individual auteurs to a collection of films unified by their use of apartment dwellings as settings for horror. The modern urban apartment, where one lives alone in the midst of anonymous multitudes, cut off from any kind of meaningful human contact, serves as an exquisite metaphor for the kind of isolation central to horror film. What better setting—in one's presumably safe home—to destabilize through the techniques of horror? The border zone of horror is not reassuringly external and distant in these films. Indeed, one never has to leave the house to become embroiled in what the Royers identify as "the connections among, the interstices of, voyeurism, paranoia, and alienation." By way of example, the Royers then embark on close readings of seven films, including Alfred Hitchcock's *Rear Window* (1954); Roman Polanski's *Repulsion* (1965), *Rosemary's Baby* (1968), and *The Tenant* (1976); David Cronenberg's *Shivers* (1975); and David Lynch's *Eraserhead* (1977) and *Blue Velvet* (1986). In these films, the need for human connection, when thwarted and distorted by modern alienation, takes on pathological dimensions within the walls of one's own home.

Of course, in horror film, the threat often comes from the external—an invasion from afar. In Chapter 6, the Royers scrutinize the ultimate cosmic Others in horror film: angels and aliens. Angels and aliens, sometimes benign entities in films such as *It's a Wonderful Life* (1946) and *E.T.* (1982), become monstrous invaders in the *Prophecy* and *Alien* series. Capable of both "miracle and mayhem," angels and aliens in horror film are reflections of the human inner self. The warring angels of *The Prophecy* (1995) and the homesick angels of *Dogma* (1999) who wish to destroy creation in order to go home to heaven are allegorical representations of the adrift, isolated human spirit in conflict with the cosmos. In science-fiction/horror films such as *The Day the Earth Stood Still* (1951) and *The War of the Worlds* (1953), the aliens who come to earth employ different methods to control humanity for different ends, but the films are similar in that the aliens possess quasi-divine powers before which humanity is helpless. A later entry in the alien invader cycle, *Fire in the Sky* (1993), presents a more localized but in its own way even more terrifying invasion—the abduction of lone human beings for incomprehensible pseudomedical bodily penetrations. When humanity leaves the earth to go out into the cosmos, the lonely travelers fare no better in films such as *Alien* (1979), in which a powerful entity from unfathomably far reaches of space becomes, for all intents and purposes, the Angel of Death.

As this quick overview indicates, the Royers discuss a number of filmmakers and specific themes (primarily those dealing with isolation) within the horror genre to create a markedly different kind of scholarly analysis—one that celebrates the resistance of horror cinema to easy definitions, rigid categories, and binary oppositions. Personally and professionally, I thank the Royers for this contribution to the study of horror.

Philip L. Simpson, PhD
Professor, English and Humanities,
and Chair, Department of Liberal Arts,
Brevard Community College, Palm Bay, Florida;
Executive Board Member, Popular Culture Association;
Editorial Board, Journal of Popular Culture

Preface

Studies of both classic and contemporary horror films have long appealed to academic and general readers alike. Many books deal with a specific subgenre, such as the vampire film, the zombie film, or the slasher film. Others focus on one actor—Vincent Price, Boris Karloff, and Christopher Lee spring to mind—or one director, exemplified by books about the films of Alfred Hitchcock and Wes Craven. As well, numerous comprehensive film histories, guides, trivia collections, and topical indexes are available. Among more scholarly studies, some take a cultural approach, others a philosophical or psychological approach. *The Spectacle of Isolation in Horror Films: Dark Parades* departs from these sorts of texts by exploring the work of several important directors in depth *and* addressing key themes of horror films, across the work of several directors and across decades. The chapters are intended to be discrete and self-sufficient, yet they also link together to form an investigation of the way common themes—such as isolation and alienation, death and transformation—shape a fairly coherent ethos in horror cinema. Although there are separate chapters on Alfred Hitchcock, Sam Raimi, and David Cronenberg, these directors' films crop up in the more theme-oriented discussions as well, in chapters on the interplay between avant-garde cinema and horror B flicks, the apartment as the cell of horror, and angels and aliens as the supernatural Other. We hope that this organization has created a more associative and imaginative approach to horror film studies than if we had been strictly theory-centric in approaching our criticism.

Acknowledgments

This book grew out of a half dozen or so presentations that we gave jointly at annual Popular Culture Association conferences. We are indebted to the Horror Area chair, Phil Simpson, for supporting our work over the years. Having that venue for our ideas and gaining input from conference participants showed us that a wider audience might be interested in a collection of horror film criticism such as that assembled here.

Thanks are also due to Lee Sanders and Pete Martin, the administrators at Miami University who granted Diana's research leave, without which this project would have taken much, much longer. We appreciate the thoughtful input of friends who watched and discussed some of the films with us, especially Jordan Max and Brian Nealon.

Last, heartfelt thanks go out to our respective parents and siblings for indulging—even encouraging—our involvement with horror films at an early age. This book really began with a young boy's fascination for watching his older brother's 8-mm reel-to-reel silent movies, and with a young girl's obsessive watching, along with her older sister, of Saturday afternoon's weekly *Creature Feature* flick.

Chapter 1

Body Doubles and Severed Hands: The Relation Between Avant-Garde Cinema and Horror Movies

Film has done more to dissolve the boundaries between high and low culture than any other medium in modern and postmodern times. One of the most compelling examples is the interplay between avant-garde "art" films and exploitation B movies, particularly of the horror genre. Both types employ low-budget production values and even tend to lose their potency as the budgets increase. Because the aesthetic intentions between the two types differ, viewers and critics tend to separate them in ways that obscure the myriad similarities they share. B movies provide shock imagery to titillate and thrill the viewer, while the avant-garde film uses similar imagery to jolt the viewer out of complacency and to alter his or her perception of reality. A close look at surrealist films will reveal that later avant-garde and horror vehicles share a common ancestry.

Surrealist avant-garde film is a term to which the surrealists themselves would have objected, since avant-garde to them meant, primarily, the films of French impressionist directors. The surrealists deemed this cinematic art "bourgeois," and thus they looked down upon the work of such directors as Louis Delluc, Marcel L'Herbier, and Jean Epstein (Kuenzli, 1987). They disdained impressionists' use of "slow-motion effects, double exposures, and moody contrasts in lighting" (Gazetas, 2000: 78) and deemed avant-garde film to be "a technique-oriented, aesthetic-dominated form" (Matthews, 1971: 14). Since a surrealist's conception of film was as "a storehouse for visual images" that would satiate viewers' desire for "the marvelous," "[e]xactly how these images are to be assembled, and with what display of technical finesse, is therefore less important to him than that their presence be felt, providing his imagination with something it can digest

1

and transform surrealistically" (Matthews, 1971: 14-15). We take the broader definition of avant-garde, encompassing not only European experimental films made from about 1918 to 1930, but also experimental (and often noncommercial) films in any time period (Konigsberg, 1987).

Eschewing the work of avant-garde directors, surrealists were drawn to comic films, especially those by Mack Sennett, Charlie Chaplin, and Buster Keaton, and to popular French serials, specifically *Les Vampires* (1915-1916), *Fantomas* (1913-1914), and *Les Mysteres de New-York* (1915) (Kuenzli, 1987). Serials appealed to the surrealists because by nature they had an "ability to evoke and sustain a sense of mystery and suspense" (Kovács, 1980: 16). Surrealists praised the popular film genres of comedy and horror for

> illustrating the collapse of reasoning resistance, as well as disso-
> lution of various inhibitions before the onslaught of desire. Both
> these are found to be poetic forms to the degree that they demon-
> strate the necessary removal of emotional, social, and moral
> obstacles which Surrealists delight in seeing cast down. (Mat-
> thews, 1971: 9)

Humor and horror often work hand in hand, so it is not surprising that some essential elements of surrealist films found their way into subsequent horror films. "The juxtaposition of the banal and the sublime, pleasure and terror, dreams and life became the very syntax of the films," Steven Kovács (1980: 42) explains in *From Enchantment to Rage: The Story of Surrealist Cinema:* "At their best the movies operated as a series of jolts to the viewer to awaken feelings normally beyond the reach of conventional methods." So too with horror B-movie makers.

The surrealist movement in all the arts reached its height from about 1925 to 1930, retaining some of the characteristics of the preceding Dada movement: "a love of irrationality, a rejection of conventional 'civilized' values, and a contempt for restraint and 'good taste'" (Giannetti, 1976: 389). Dada films are "radically non-narrative" and "attempt to undermine the norms and codes of social conventions, and thus of conventional filmmaking" (Kuenzli, 1987: 7). Although some critics cast a wide eye on which films classify as surrealist, many of these films are more exactly dadaist. René Clair and Francis Picabia's *Entr'acte* (1924), Man Ray's *L'Étoile de Mer*

(1928), and Antonin Artaud and Germaine Dulac's *La Coquille et le Clergyman* (1928) are, arguably, more dadaist than surrealist efforts. No one, however, debates the categorization of *Un Chien Andalou* (1929) and *L'Âge d'or* (1930); they are completely surrealist. Some even claim that these two are the *only* surrealist films.

Un Chien Andalou, directed by Luis Buñuel from a scenario by Buñuel and Salvador Dalí, perhaps best illustrates the division between art cinema and B movies as well as what elements would cross over from surrealist into horror films. Buñuel and Dalí had an acrimonious dispute over how much credit belonged to whom, but given Dalí's mania for self-promotion and calculated disregard for fact, Buñuel's version seems more believable. Dalí alleged that "he presented Buñuel with a complete alternative scenario, scribbled in a quarter of an hour on a shoe-box" (Drummond, 1994: ix)—"alternative" because Buñuel had a different setting in mind for the film, that of the newspaper world. Dalí's shoebox claim has a nice surrealistic air to it, but the scenario seems to have been written over the course of a little more than a week while Buñuel was visiting Dalí. Later in life Buñuel recalled that while writing the script, he and Dalí "never had the slightest disagreement; we spent a week of total identification" (Drummond, 1994: 104). Steven Kovács (1980) studied letters and autobiography to delve into this issue of each artist's contribution and came to the conclusion that Dalí's role in writing the scenario was "considerable," while his involvement with shooting the film was "much more limited" (185). Buñuel (1994) notes that the filming took two weeks and that "Dalí arrived on the set a few days before the end and spent most of his time pouring wax into the eyes of stuffed donkeys" (104-105). Kovács (1980) observes also that images in both *Un Chien Andalou* and *L'Âge d'or* "can be said to belong to both men's artistic repertoires," such as the donkey carcass and the hand with ants crawling on it (190). What is indisputable is that the pair, in writing the scenario for *Un Chien Andalou,* adhered to strict surrealist practices. In his autobiography, *My Last Breath,* Buñuel (1994) writes,

> No idea or image that might lend itself to a rational explanation of any kind would be accepted. We had to open all doors to the irrational and keep only those images that surprised us, without trying to explain why. (104)

The two employed images from their dreams, of course, and what they began with are among the most infamous shock images in all of cinema, comparable to the shower scene in Alfred Hitchcock's *Psycho* (1960) and the initial zombie assault in George A. Romero's *Night of the Living Dead* (1968). The film opens with a visceral reflexivity: A man sharpens a straight razor; a thin cloud drifts in front of a full moon; the razor slices a woman's eye. Of all the eye motifs in film history, this one is the most assaulting to the viewer; Buñuel claimed that he himself was repelled the first few times he watched the scene (although he did a fine job acting as the character who does the slicing). At the time the film was made Georges Bataille attributed the scene to Dalí, while in later years Buñuel claimed this image to be his contribution (Kovács, 1980: 191). *Un Chien Andalou,* Buñuel (1994) writes in his autobiography, "came from an encounter between two dreams" (103). While visiting Dalí, he continues,

> I told him about a dream I'd had in which a long, tapering cloud sliced the moon in half, like a razor blade slicing through an eye. Dalí immediately told me that he'd seen a hand crawling with ants in a dream he'd had the previous night. (Buñuel, 1994: 103-104)

The image of ants crawling around in a hole in the palm of a hand is less abusive than that of an eye being sliced, but equally memorable. Since the scenario was written in a collaborative, amiable manner, it might be best to downplay specific contributions. At any rate, attribution is far less an issue with *L'Âge d'or.* Trying again to write a scenario together, Buñuel found that the "magical rapport" of the earlier collaboration was gone, so he wrote the screenplay himself, including in it a few ideas Dalí sent him (Buñuel, 1994). Dalí did not attend the filming and observed in his autobiography, *The Secret Life of Salvador Dalí,* "Buñuel was going ahead all by himself with the production of *L'Âge d'or*—thus the film would be executed without my collaboration" (Dalí, 1993: 276-77).

Un Chien Andalou, all seventeen-odd minutes of it, abounds in visual puns and outright silliness, but even the most humorous moments are infected by a keen sense of the macabre. Buñuel's fascination with severed limbs first manifests itself here: A hand lies in the street, and an androgynous girl nudges it with a stick, as if it were a dead rat. The severed hand with a life of its own would, of course, become a mainstay of the horror genre, culminating in the gleefully demented appendage that tries to kill its erstwhile owner in Sam Raimi's *Evil Dead II* (1987). Clearly the subject touches a nerve.

A later image in *Un Chien Andalou* has also worked its way into the horror bag of tricks. At one point the protagonist (Pierre Batcheff) wipes his hand across his mouth and, voilà, his mouth vanishes. The woman in the scene (Simone Mareuil) pointedly applies her lipstick while glancing at him. Similar disappearing mouths have appeared in various movies, including a segment of *Twilight Zone: The Movie* (1983), where a young boy has the ability to make happen what he imagines, and he imagines that his sister's mouth disappears. Perhaps the original surrealist version was even the stimulus for author Harlan Ellison's most inspired title, *I Have No Mouth and I Must Scream* (1967). Both frustration and horror are implied by that title, and the subtext of the vanishing mouth is that one is cut off from humanity. Not only is there the loss of verbal expression of one's self as an individual, the interaction with others through conversation, and an intimate connection through kissing—sustenance cannot be taken in; one will wither and die.

For all the insistent bizarreness of images in *Un Chien Andalou*, there is an underlying poetic quality to much of the film, a sensibility more in keeping with Buñuel's oeuvre than with Dalí's. Indeed, Buñuel once referred to the following description of the poetic effect of cinema:

> J.B. Brunius draws our attention to the fact that the darkness that gradually invades the auditorium is the same as closing the eyes: next, on the screen, and within man, the darkness of unconsciousness begins to make inroads; as in the dream, the images appear and disappear by means of dissolves or fades-in and -out; time and space become flexible, contract and stretch at will, chronological order and relative values of duration no longer correspond to reality; cyclical action may elapse in a few minutes or in several centuries; the movements speed up; the time lags. (Buñuel, 2000: 114)

Buñuel (2000) called the cinema "an instrument of poetry, with all that this word possesses of a liberating sense, of a subversion of reality, of a threshold at the marvelous world of the subconscious, of a nonconformity with the mean-spirited society surrounding us" (112).

Given his views, it is appropriate that Buñuel's poetry has an ironic bent. One critic has explained, "The nature of Buñuelian irony has direct bearing on certain metaphors in the film, often ascribed to Dalí," such as the books held in each hand of the protagonist with his arms held out to the side, elbows bent; the books become pistols (Finkelstein, 1987: 137). Whereas "Dalí appears to amuse himself " with "irrational speculations," the images contributed by Buñuel "embody a sense of violence and cruelty, and are often derisively anti-religious, even blasphemous, in their mixing of eroticism with sacred symbols" (Finkelstein, 1987: 136). The man's stance suggests the crucifixion, a holy image that is undercut when the books transform into weapons that the man, who had been standing with his nose against the wall in punishment, uses to shoot his punisher, who bears a strange resemblance to himself. Incidentally, the doppelgänger comes out of the Gothic tradition in literature—Edgar Allan Poe used it to great effect in his psychological tales of terror—and became a horror-film convention.

At the end of *Un Chien Andalou,* a happy couple strolls along a rocky beach, a title card reads "In the Spring," and the final shot is a still of the couple, now in a desert, buried up to their chests in the sand. The film quality makes it hard to verify, but the shooting script indicates that large winged insects surround them (Buñuel and Dalí, 1994): a poetic, disquieting image that indicates life even as it depicts death.

Obviously *Un Chien Andalou* is not a horror movie in the sense of F. W. Murnau's version of the Dracula myth, *Nosferatu* (1922)—which was rescreened in Paris from 1928 to 1929 and admired by the surrealists (Matthews, 1971)—or Fritz Lang's profile of a child-murderer, *M* (1931), both of which are also highly artful films. *Un Chien Andalou*'s goals are clearly different. Not only is it nonlinear; it is positively antinarrative. It seeks to be a cracked funhouse mirror, piling distortion on distortion, bewilderment on bewilderment. In that regard it seems closer to a certain vein of maverick horror filmmaking than Murnau's or Lang's subtler masterpieces—to such movies as those by Italian auteur Dario Argento, who gave viewers *Suspiria* (1977), or Sam Raimi's *Evil Dead* trilogy (discussed at length in Chapter 3). In a way, it seems a common ancestor of certain radical art films such as Ingmar Bergman's *Hour of the Wolf* (1968), Andrei Tarkovsky's *Stalker* (1979), and David Lynch's *Eraserhead* (1977).

All of these films toy almost recklessly with linear narrative, and all use shocking or disturbing imagery to create a sensory dislocation in the viewer.

One other element that links all of those films is a celebration of fetishization. Critics have labeled Buñuel as any number of fetishistic "types": shoe, child, Christ, et cetera. More to the point, he fetishized fetishism itself. He played with different perversions and taboos as a method to liberate the unconscious, the irrational, and the poetry of chaos. The surrealist attitude, more than one critic has observed, "is one of revulsion for the limitations imposed by society upon the free play of feeling. It denotes rebellion against the controls imposed and maintained in our relationships with other people" (Matthews, 1971: 8). What better approach than to focus on the physical aspects of love and its attendant obsessions, compulsions, and, in some people's view, perversions?

Sometimes Buñuel accomplished this liberation of the unconscious via fetishes rather comically. In his second film, *L'Âge d'or,* he rampantly fetishized everything from maniacal cruelty to toe sucking (one character even sucks the toes of a statue); if John Waters were Spanish, he might have created this film. Indeed, he might have titled it *God's Wicked Little Acre.* The film begins with scorpions fighting, a short insect documentary that could be correlated with human behavior, and soon moves on to four bishops on a rocky cliff above the sea, chanting ceremonially, if impassively—symbolically ossified, as they would indeed actually become a bit later in the film. A lookout bandit returns from higher on the cliff to his ragged group, and they struggle through a rugged landscape toward the sea, dying one by one. Only the skeletons of the bishops remain by this point, and a large party including clergy, public officials, and military officers lands on the beach to pay their respect to the bishops' remains. They then conduct a ceremony to found a new civilization. But for all these seemingly random, outré juxtapositions, most of the action of *L'Âge d'or* concerns an insular group of bourgeoisie and the endlessly frustrated attempts of the protagonist (Gaston Modot)—a deranged, obsessed sadist—to get together with a willing but elusive woman (Lya Lys). This begins when the couple rolls passionately in the mud as the ceremony is about to commence. The mud and other feces-related images in the film are suggestive of "the perverse erotic syndrome of coprophilia" (Weiss, 1987: 160).

Although the lovers are kept apart by society (the woman is escorted from the scene, followed by nuns, and the man is dragged off by the police), Buñuel delivers a variety of images and motifs that connect the two, such as cutting from an advertisement's photograph of a seductive woman that the man spots to a shot of his lover holding her head in a similar pose. Each character chews his or her bottom lip as a sign of raging passion for the other. Most amusing is the large cow the woman finds on her bed, whose bell tinkles as it is chased off, allowing Buñuel to connect the lovers through sound as well as imagery: cow bell and dogs' barking are heard by each, even though the man and woman are in different locations.

After a grueling day in which the man struggles to reunite with the woman (that he kicks a dog, squashes an insect, and kicks over a blind man during the course of the day indicates his sadistic nature as much as his sexual frustration), the two end up at the same party, in company with members of high society. The soiree setting, for Buñuel and others who have used it, is

> an appropriate symbol because it features the most successful members of society meeting simply in order to amuse themselves, but who do so in a highly formal, rigid manner. It illustrates the absurd extreme of the socialization process, a structuring of behavior in a situation set up precisely in order to allow personal relaxation. (Kovács, 1980: 220)

Buñuel criticizes these straight-laced members of society in vivid ways: the host's face is covered with flies, guests ignore a farm cart containing drunken workers as it passes through the ballroom, and they pay little attention when the gamekeeper shoots his son to death in a field. As Steven Kovács (1980) points out, "It matters precious little when the child of a worker is killed outside, but when social decorum is violated in the ballroom, it calls for moral outrage on the part of everyone" (221): just after the shooting, the protagonist arrives and the hostess (who is his lover's mother) accidentally spills a drink on him. It is as much his fault as it is hers, but he nonetheless slaps her quite hard and is thrown out of the party.

Driven by lust, he returns to seek his lover, and the ensuing scenes demonstrate the additional interruptions of society into their attempts at lovemaking, primarily out in the garden. They do finally embrace, but the man is distracted by the toes on a statue, and when he is summoned into the house to take a telephone call, the woman sucks the statue's toes in a fetishistic connection with her lover's desires. The two fondle and embrace each other after the man returns, but inexplicably the woman throws herself at the orchestra conductor, who has been performing at the party, when he wanders onto the scene. The protagonist rushes alone to the woman's bedroom and, completely frustrated sexually as well as anguished over her abandonment, throws several incongruous items out of a window: a burning tree, a bishop, a ploughshare, the bishop's crook, and an artificial giraffe (which, unlike the previous items, falls into a body of water). The very last item, feathers from the woman's bed pillow he has ripped open, becomes the snow banks surrounding the chateau "where four godless libertines, led by the Duke of Blangy, retired for 120 days to celebrate the most brutal of orgies"—a reference to *120 Days of Sodom* by the Marquis de Sade, which is "an encyclopedic fictional compendium of the perverse manifestations of desire" (Weiss, 1987: 166-167). In a truly surrealistic move, Buñuel initially has the character of the duke resemble Christ. As Kovács (1980) remarks, "Surely there was no better way to cap the ridicule and criticism [Buñuel] leveled at the Church throughout the film. In this final passage he drives home his point that the values of bourgeois society are completely reversed" (227). Dalí's (1993) response to the film was, "I was terribly disappointed, for it was but a caricature of my ideas. The 'Catholic' side of it had become crudely anticlerical, and without the biological poetry that I had desired" (282).

J. H. Matthews delves into Buñuel's intent to offer an insightful explanation of the important development of surrealist filmmaking that occurred even in the short time between the making of these two films:

> The director's purpose in *Un Chien Andalou* was to sever consciously perceived connections between succeeding images and sequences. It is much more characteristic of his method in *L'Âge d'or,* though, that sequences and individual shots are connected in such a way as to oblige the spectator to draw conclusions which will influence his view of life. Buñuel intends to control viewer reaction here far more directly than in *Un Chien Andalou.* His intention is evidenced in his shooting script by the prominence given effects plainly designed to elicit anticipated

responses, no less by use of sound than by arrangement of images. (Matthews, 1971: 97)

The result is a more cohesive moral statement. Buñuel "takes the theme of psychosexual drives from *Un Chien Andalou* and locates them in a social context" in *L'Âge d'or,* thereby studying humans in relation to one another (Kovács, 1980: 211). Linda Williams (1981), too, sees *L'Âge d'or* as "very much a continuation of the Surrealist exploration of the structure of desire begun in *Un Chien Andalou;* it is simply given a different elaboration and emphasis in the later film" (109). Whereas the first film concerns the "illusory unity of the self," the second concerns the "illusory unity of the social body" (Williams, 1981:109). Buñuel does indeed achieve a greater study of sexual drives and society's attitudes on this issue, as well as others, in the second film.

Not long after these two seminal films, surrealistically enough, Tod Browning's *Freaks* (1932) would present a mirror situation of the one in *L'Âge d'or.* In Browning's film, the insular group are the low ones—the circus freaks—while the transgressive couple are outwardly normal and inwardly warped and sociopathic. "The tradition of exploitation film making," John McCarty explains in *The Sleaze Merchants,* "extends all the way back to the silent era when independent producers ground out pictures dealing with sensational subjects—poverty, race, drugs, prostitution, and so on—[that] their Hollywood counterparts either considered beneath them or just too hot to handle" (1995: viii). *Freaks* is an exploitation movie in the fullest sense of the term: a low-budget B film dealing with a taboo subject, the visceral horror of deformed and bizarre-looking human beings. In addition, it uses actual performers from freak shows, which in itself is surreal. However, these so-called freaks are depicted with remarkable compassion and even tenderness; the film never treats them with condescension.

At age sixteen, Browning ran off to work as a carny, and this no doubt provided the experience for him to deeply empathize with the sideshow oddities. Exploitation cinema boasts a number of filmmakers who started in the carny milieu, including David F. Friedman, producer of *She Freak* (1967)—a remake of Browning's *Freaks*—although no other movie, outside of David Lynch's *The Elephant Man* (1980), portrays freaks so warmly, subtly, and with such poetic resonance. Nearly every scene in *Freaks* conveys a delicacy of emotion, an appreciation of the special culture these people developed, and a fascination with the way they compensated for their physical limitations that shows no trace of morbidity; rather, it shows admiration and compassion. When viewers see an armless and legless "human torso" light a cigar with his teeth, they are neither horrified nor disgusted. Instead, they fall under a spell of contemplation, both at the ingenuity and skill of the maneuver and at the human torso's obvious enjoyment of one of life's simple pleasures.

The pivotal theme of the movie is the freaks' self-contained, self-enforcing subculture, complete with a "code of ethics to protect them from the barbs of normal people," as an opening title card informs viewers. The central tenet of the code is, "Offend one, and you offend all," a protective rule that leads to the antagonists' downfall. Actually, these two "normal" humans come across as so monstrous that when the freaks turn to brutal vengeance the viewers' sympathy falls completely to the latter. They have been driven to this retaliation by the normal world's cruelty.

The normal woman, a trapeze artist named Cleopatra (Olga Baclanova), and her strongman boyfriend, Hercules (Henry Victor), are, of course, the true freaks because of their corrupt, venomous souls. When Cleo learns that the midget Hans (Harry Earles), whom she toys with mockingly, is coming into an inheritance, she pursues him in earnest until she becomes his wife. At their nuptial celebration, "Cuckoo" the Chicken Woman dances on the table, a sword swallower demonstrates his skills, and the pinheads giggle with glee. As a midget takes around a chalice of wine for all to sip from, the gathered freaks welcome Cleo into the fold by chanting, "We accept her! One of us, one of us. Gooble gobble." Her response is one of the most spectacular losses of composure in cinematic history. She screams, "No! Slime! Freaks!" and then tosses wine from the communal chalice in the little toastmaster's face. She orders the guests to leave, then belittles Hans, her diminutive betrothed, by taunting him: "Must I play games with you? Must Momma take you horsey-back ride?"

Cleo had begun poisoning Hans at the party, and, after a doctor sees him because Hans collapsed, Cleo continues to add poison to the prescribed remedy. But the midget toastmaster spies through the window and later joins with Hans and the other freaks in planning revenge. The entire film breathes an irrational, dreamlike quality, and this reaches its height in the scene where, with mounting tension, the caravan of circus wagons moves through the rainy night to the next town. Hans and his friends extract the vial of poison from Cleo while, in another wagon, Hercules tries to kill Venus (Leila Hyams), one of the circus' managers, who suspected Cleo and Hercules of plotting to murder Hans for his fortune. Wagons careen over; Hercules receives a knife in the back from a midget and lies in the mud watching as a band of freaks—a pinhead, midgets, the human torso—all crawl steadily toward him to enforce their code by finishing him off. Browning cuts to Cleo running into the woods, screaming, chased by another group of freaks.

Freaks is a tremendously artful movie. The Grand Guignol ending, however repulsive, is built up to with an almost classical sense of structure, using a framing device that is both suspenseful and elegant. The film opens with a circus barker gently reprimanding the crowd for laughing and shuddering at the freaks they have seen. "But for the accident of birth, you might be even as they are," he says soberly, which introduces Browning's avant-garde undermining of the accepted social and cultural norms of the middle and upper classes: One's physical appearance is *not* indicative of one's moral nature; deformity should not exclude one from the privileges of the normal. "You are about to witness the most amazing, the most astounding living monstrosity of all times," the barker notes, taking the crowd over to a large bin into which they, but not the audience, can see. A woman screams and turns away. The barker begins telling the monstrosity's story: "She was once a beautiful woman. . . ." Browning cuts to a shot of Cleo on her trapeze as the man's voice fades out and circus music fades in. At the end of the film, Browning returns to the barker and crowd, who are looking into the bin. "Some say a jealous lover, others that it was the code of the freaks, others, the storm," the barker relates dramatically. Viewers then see that Cleo, once known as the "peacock of the air," has been turned into a chicken lady, covered with feathers, her face deformed, squawking rather than talking, and apparently legless, for she is now as short as a midget. Cleo had once ridiculed the freaks and felt herself superior to them because of her normalcy. She has been humbled in one of the most horrifying lessons depicted in cinema.

Another B movie would have ended there, with the horn section swelling, but here we get a final, moving scene: Hans's true love, his fellow midget Frieda (Daisy Earles), comes to him in his familial mansion to reconcile and tells him, "It was only the poison you wanted. It wasn't your fault." Order is restored, and the fragile society of the freaks gains strength through their unified attack on evil, the "poison" embodied in the woman with a normal body. Browning tells a moving, if melodramatic, story that happens to exploit the public's fascination with the grotesque and the macabre.

While schlockmeister Herschell Gordon Lewis was creating the splatter-film subgenre with such masterworks as *Blood Feast* (1963) and *2,000 Maniacs* (1964), films of such dubious quality that only a true surrealist (or a full-blown wackaloon) could love them, Alfred Hitchcock delivered *Psycho,* a low-budget serial-killer movie that was one of his most sophisticated, at least visually. In fact, its shower scene ends with another of the most famous eye motifs: the pan-in on the still shot of Marion's (Janet Leigh's) open, dead eye, her lashes glistening, a drop of water—or is it a tear?—sliding down her nose.

That murder, the most sensational scene in the film, points to the eccentric nature of *Psycho*'s structure: The narrative arc is skewed throughout, as emphasized by Bernard Herrmann's modernist score, a kind of symphonic porcupine. *Psycho* actually consists of two related stories; the first ends with Marion's death and the still image of her eye, and the second with Norman Bates's (Anthony Perkins) exposure as the murderer, followed by a tagged-on pseudopsychological explanation of his behavior.

Hitchcock explored some of his most innovative and unusual cinematographical techniques here, manipulating the camera in such a way as to make the viewer anxiously complicit in the onscreen crimes. When Norman puts his fingers to his lips, waiting for the car and corpse to sink, viewers might reflexively do the same; at the least, most share his little-boy relief when the vehicle disappears from view. And so, just as Browning made the freaks' "code of ethics" sympathetic, and just as Buñuel threw out conventional morals entirely, Hitchcock drops viewers almost seductively into Mama Bates's lap by evoking their sympathy for the mother-obsessed son.

A worthwhile side note: Tobe Hooper's *The Texas Chainsaw Massacre* (1974) was based on the same real-life case as *Psycho,* equally loosely. Ed Gein was one of the most pitiable of all murderers. The reclusive Wisconsin farmer lived with his puritanical mother until he was middle aged. After both his parents were dead, the physical abuse he had suffered from his father and the sexual repression inherited from his mother erupted. From Gein's hollow life, Robert Bloch took the mother fixation for his 1959 novel *Psycho* (always a favorite subtext of Hitchcock's as well) and Hooper took Gein's hobbies of cannibalism and tanning human skins. There is also a compelling docudrama on Gein, directed by Chuck Parello, simply titled *Ed Gein* (2000) and starring Steve Railsback as the killer and Carrie Snodgress as his mother. Sometimes the deadest of eyes have a lot of life to give. As Philip L. Simpson notes in *Psycho Paths: Tracking the Serial Killer Through Contemporary American Film and Fiction,* serial killers "are slowly metamorphosing into immortal (and profitable) cultural icons" (2000: 2). He suggests that

> in our attempt to understand serial killers, we inevitably create myths about them—works of fiction that may superficially portray the serial killer as the ultimate alien outsider or enemy of society but which simultaneously reflect back upon society its own perversions, fears, and murderous desires. Thus, the serial killer is "psycho"—aberrant and depraved—while still remaining a recognizable product of American culture. (2000: 1-2)

The exploitation aspect of serial killer movies is rooted in the larger genre of texts about death, especially death at the hands of another. Society's fears and obsessions are indeed at the core in all of these texts, perhaps most so in those dealing with serial killers because such stories emphasize the unpredictable and random nature of mortality (Royer, 2003). Filmmakers exploit the particular serial killer taken as their subject, but they exploit their viewers' emotions as well.

As cinema developed through the twentieth century, distinctions between art and exploitation became harder and harder to divine, as can be seen in the works of George A. Romero, John Waters, and David Cronenberg. Late in the 1960s, Romero's *Night of the Living Dead* trounced any remnant of sympathy for most human life with the force of a jackboot. But while the film is as cynical and violent as a Herschell Gordon Lewis gore fest, it is the cynicism of a lapsed idealist and the violence of an artist deeply concerned with and disgusted by contemporary world events: lynch mobs, Vietnam, plaid hunting jackets, and the middle-American "patriotic" values they represent. Romero started out making a low-budget zombie flick, the gravy on the exploitation biscuit, and ended up with a kind of Venusian caviar—a movie that belongs to a ghetto subgenre, the zombie flick, yet mesmerizes the willing viewer in a way reminiscent of the best Bergman films: strange and repulsive, yet with a lingering aftertaste of near genius. Romero would refine this talent through the years, with mixed results.

Night of the Living Dead is a strikingly sophisticated movie visually, considering that it was Romero's first feature and a low-budget genre film. (The seed money was $60,000, with $54,000 deferred until it was released [Romero, 1974].) It employs chiaroscuro, noir-style lighting to emphasize humanity's nightmare alienation from itself. As Romero wrote, "The film opens with a situation that has already disintegrated to a point of little hope, and it moves progressively toward absolute despair and ultimate tragedy" (1974: 5).

A group of strangers hole up in a farm house and attempt to defend themselves against the living dead, recently dead humans whose brains have become animated and who have "an urge to kill other humans and devour their flesh," as a news commentator reports. The ostensible explanation is that a rocket ship sent toward Venus brought high-level radiation with it when it returned to earth. The cause matters little to the group of humans trying to survive an onslaught of the living dead, and Romero effectively depicts the disintegration of the microsociety within the farmhouse. One is uselessly comatose at the shock of her brother being killed by a ghoul; two who try to cooperate with Ben (Duane Jones), the natural leader of the endeavor because he is the most level-headed thinker, get blown up in a truck that all hoped would offer escape; a child-turned-ghoul feasts on her father's body after Ben is forced to shoot him for impeding the survival efforts, then kills her mother with a trowel. Ben, the only survivor over the course of the night, hears rescuers approaching the house and peeks out, only to be shot dead because he is taken for a ghoul. Given the time period in which the film was made, it seems justifiable to extract deep meaning from this murder of the only character played by a black actor, and the one truly heroic character. But Romero has stated that Jones was chosen for the role because he was the best actor who auditioned. This and other decisions, such as using black-and-white film because it was less expensive than color, contributed accidentally to the film's enduring reputation. As Romero describes it, "Our own relaxed, honest, uninhibited, naive attitudes as we approached the production ultimately read-out as unconscious elements in the picture which added to its realism, offhandedness and uniqueness" (1974: 11). Accident, craft, and a bunch of animal innards provided by an investor made *Night of the Living Dead* an avant-garde horror film cult classic.

In contrast to the dim lighting and night setting of the first movie, the later *Dawn of the Dead* (1978) shows almost every atrocity in broad daylight or the bright lights of the shopping mall that serves as its main setting. The light shines on both the living and the undead, and the avant-garde aspects lie in the glaring depictions of unspeakable horrors, such as when a zombie's scalp is cleanly hewn by a helicopter's blades, or when, under the cold fluorescent lights of the shopping mall's storage rooms, a SWAT officer must shoot his companion officer and best friend, who has become a zombie through his own hubris. The movie presents such vile images almost to the point of overload, yet it creates a mood that is hypnotic, even beguiling. The third installment, *Day of the Dead* (1985), is to zombie flicks what *The Godfather Part III* (1990) is to gangster movies: irrelevant, tedious, and wholly misguided. The setting this time is an underground military complex, the intended object of satire swinging from mindless consumerism, as was the target in *Dawn of the Dead,* back to politics of various sorts, the target in *Night of the Living Dead.* Any praise for the film generally goes to Tom Savini for the gore and unparalleled zombie makeup.

From the 1970s on, exploitation subjects were co-opted by the major Hollywood studios. The drive-in sensationalism of cannibals and serial killers became big-budget thriller material, ranging from such masterworks as *The Silence of the Lambs* (1991) to such dreck as *Copycat* (1995). Ultimately, Hollywood, rather than history, is the nightmare from which we cannot escape. Yet there is hope: various filmmakers have managed to fuse avant-garde, exploitation, and horror aspects in new and engaging ways, both within the studio system and on its borders, with varying degrees of success. The great Canadian master David Cronenberg, for example, who is discussed at length in Chapter 4, is well on his way to having created the most prodigious and disturbing body of work in cinematic history.

Although fundamentally a satirist, John Waters in his early work mines a vein between the risible and the unspeakable. He has acknowledged his love of the gore films of Herschell Gordon Lewis, as well as his guilty pleasure of art films, particularly those by Ingmar Bergman and Rainer Werner Fassbinder. An observation about the early surrealist filmmakers might be applied to his work, that "their montage of incongruous sequences aimed at breaking open the spectator's unconscious drives and obsessions. Cinematographic techniques were thus only a means to disrupt the symbolic order, and to let the unconscious erupt" (Kuenzli, 1987: 9). In movies such as *Multiple Maniacs* (1970), *Pink Flamingos* (1972), *Female Trouble* (1974), and *Desperate Living* (1977), Waters creates a fantastical world of fetishism and alternate morality, as for instance when, in *Pink Flamingos,* the highest goal in life for the characters is to be "the filthiest people alive." Everyone talks about the infamous dog turd-eating scene, but it is actually one of the least offensive moments in the film. The forced insemination of kidnapped young women with a turkey baster seems more provocative; it is a scene at which even Buñuel might have balked.

Likewise, Divine's rape by a giant lobster at the climax of *Multiple Maniacs* beautifully combines the giant-creature B movies of the 1950s with surrealist conceptions of the irrational; it is *Them!* (1954) crossed with *L'Âge d'or,* a combination of silliness and high-minded satire. One watches with unsettling ambivalence, uncertain whether to laugh at the absurdity of the situation or to be appalled at the violation (performed by a fake lobster on an obvious transvestite). In Waters's early films humor and horror skip hand in hand, or teeter on a seesaw. Sometimes the most brutal scenes are, anarchically, the funniest, as when in *Desperate Living* a rebuffed transsexual cuts off her new penis because of her lover's disgust. In other scenes, such as when the mutilated Divine opens fire on a fashion-show crowd at the climax of *Female Trouble,* amusing satire descends into an amoral provocation to violence. This fulfills, at least in fantasy, André Breton's famous dictum that the ultimate surrealist act would be to shoot randomly into a crowd of people. Referring to the terrorist who assassinated Rajiv Ghandi, Waters explained that his fascination with that action lies in his inability to comprehend it (Ives, 1992).

Despite his reputation as a monger of trash, filth, degradation, et cetera, John Waters is at heart an earnest and honest boy, much like Buñuel. He is loyal to his friends and faithful to his family. (*Shock Value: A Tasteful Book About Bad Taste* features a charming photo of him with his grandmother.) He has a work ethic equal to any other director and certainly surpassing that of the average writer. And he ensures that his movies show a profit, because, as he has indicated, the financial success of a film lets him make another (Ives, 1992). He is a model example of the Great American Eccentric, somewhere between Joseph Cornell and Charles Manson.

David Lynch too could be labeled a contemporary surrealist who, like Waters, thrusts elements of American life before his viewers only to peel back the placid veneer and expose the rottenness that lies beneath the surface. (His *Eraserhead* and *Blue Velvet* [1986] are discussed in Chapter 5.) Both the television series *Twin Peaks* (1990) and the movie *Twin Peaks: Fire Walk with Me* (1992) concern the taboo subject of parent-child incest, served up with various horror elements that resonate all the more because of the quirky humor they are set beside. The focal point for exploring the lives of Twin Peaks' residents and visitors is the mysterious murder of Laura Palmer (Sheryl Lee), a prom queen who took meals to shut-ins but who also engaged in such activities as drinking at a club and brothel named One-Eyed Jack's. Special Agent Dale Cooper (Kyle MacLachlan) investigates her murder, and viewers ultimately discover that the killer is Laura's father, Leland (Ray Wise), who, because he was inhabited by "Bob" (Frank Silva), had been forcing his daughter to have sexual relations with him. Lynch, whose cowriter on the television series was Mark Frost, calls Bob "an abstraction with a human form" who is all the more "unnerving" because he appears in daylight (cited in Rodley, 1997: 178, 179). Such terrors are nighttime visitors in traditional horror films. *Twin Peaks* includes "some pretty strange and violent things," to use Lynch's own description (cited in Rodley, 1997: 179). "If it's not quite standard it sneaks through," he explains about their lack of censorship, "but it could be that the 'not quite standard' things make it even more terrifying and disturbing: the kind of thing they don't have names for" (cited in Rodley, 1997: 178).

This would include a psychopomp known as the Man from Another Place (Michael Anderson), a midget whom Agent Cooper encounters in the Red Room of the Black Lodge that is Bob's abode, a kind of alternate reality accessed within a circle of twelve sycamore trees. Lynch says of the art-deco, red-curtained Red Room, "It's a free zone, completely unpredictable and therefore pretty exciting but also scary. And those kinds of places are just fantastic to visit" (cited in Rodley, 1997: 19). The director makes use of a strobe light, precise editing (in the final episode, there are frame-by-frame intercuts of Laura Palmer screaming, color with no image, and Windom Earle's [Kenneth Welsh's] face), and sound to heighten viewers' uneasiness during the Red Room scenes. The actors, Lynch says, were recorded speaking their dialogue phonetically backward, then the track was reversed, which created what Lynch describes as "a beautifully strange version of the original" (cited in Rodley, 1997: 165). In the final episode a giant appears next to the midget, saying that they are "One and the same," and Lynch does seem to be exploring an ontological dialectic in *Twin Peaks.* "Doppelgänger," the Man from Another Place says to Agent Cooper, at which point a screaming Laura Palmer moves in the same manner as Bob. Shortly after, Bob sucks the soul out of Windom Earle, then a doppelgänger Cooper chases and catches the good Agent Cooper. The Bob-inhabited, bad Agent Cooper is the one who returns to the real world.

The last episode of the *Twin Peaks* series is especially relentless in delivering appalling and devastating events, including the torture of a wife-beating thug and the accidental, probably lethal wounding of Benjamin Horne (Richard Beymer) by a kind doctor who just wants to protect his family from Horne's corrupting presence. Arguably the most jolting scene of horror is that in the bank, where Lynch departs from the usual coffee-pie-doughnut humor and the amusement of his acting the part of the deaf Agent Gordon Cole. He begins by playing the scene for comedy. Audrey Horne (Sherilyn Fenn) handcuffs herself to the bank vault's door in protest of the Ghostwood Development Project, then pertly asks the bank attendant for a drink of water. The elderly man shuffles from vault door to water cooler, to vault door, and back toward the water cooler, a slow-moving, bent-kneed human question mark. Another attendant, an older woman, sleeps at her desk throughout the entire scene. Pete Martell (Jack Nance) and a character thought to have been dead, Andrew Packard (Dan O'Herlihy), come into the room to get the contents of a safety deposit box. Slowly, confusedly, the attendant looks at the safety deposit box key through a hand-held magnifying glass, his heavy-framed eyeglasses not being up to the task without assistance. When the box is opened, a bomb is revealed, along with a little propped-up note that reads, "Got you, Andrew, Love, Thomas." It might have read, "Got you, Viewer," for a huge explosion blows out the windows of the bank, and viewers see the elderly attendant's eyeglasses flying through the air, along with five one-dollar bills—one for each of the other people killed in the blast: Audrey, the woman bank attendant, Pete, Andrew, and a security guard who had entered the room and, having just learned he was a father, had proclaimed, "It's a boy!"

Twin Peaks was cancelled midway through its second season. Lynch said that the final episode was simply what would have been shown at that point in the series. Given the intense wrenching up of brutality and psychic devastation, his claim seems disingenuous. Many of the main characters die or transmogrify into monstrosities. In truth, Lynch managed one of his serial Pyrrhic victories, in effect flipping a massive middle finger at the ABC network while also forcing it to air what is possibly the most subversive—certainly the most outré—television segment ever aired. It is as if Luis Buñuel had directed an episode of *The Twilight Zone*.

The ultimate scene shows Agent Cooper waking after his traumatic encounters in the Black Lodge. He is safe in his hotel room, being watched over by Sheriff Harry Truman (Michael Ontkean) and the doctor. "How's Annie?" he asks, inquiring about his girlfriend (Heather Graham), whom he knows Windom Earle has murdered. (Earle had earlier murdered Cooper's wife, Caroline.) Told that she is in the hospital and will be fine, he states emphatically, "I need to brush my teeth." In the bathroom, he squeezes all the toothpaste out of the tube, then butts his head into the mirror over the sink. Bob's face is the reflection. Agent Cooper begins to giggle maniacally and call out sarcastically, "How's Annie? How's Annie?" Cooper's dementia, his acid corruption, speaks volumes about Lynch's experiences with commercial television.

An intriguing return to implied terror was the triumph of *The Blair Witch Project* (1999), Daniel Myrick and Eduardo Sánchez's low-budget feature—made for less than $40,000, it garnered a box-office revenue of $130 million. The mock documentary concerns three college film students making a documentary about a local legend, the Blair Witch, and their disappearance into the woods near Burkittsville, Maryland. A year later, anthropology students find their equipment and footage buried beneath an old cabin, and this footage is what ostensibly constitutes most of the movie. Myrick and Sánchez sent their actors into the woods with camping gear, a movie camera, a VCR, and the concept of the Blair Witch, and this evoked incredible emotional reactions from them. Heather Donahue, Josh Leonard, and Mike Williams all play themselves, and although they are quite aware that they are making a film, as Paul Wells observes in *The Horror*

Genre: From Beelzebub to Blair Witch, "their real emotions and fears are exploited through the way that the film is made, thus enhancing the veracity of the horror the viewer is asked to imagine in the story they witness" (2000: 109). The essential conceit of the movie is that everything is shot from the actors' point of view. As well, whatever is terrorizing them is never seen, with the result that both actors and viewers are quite unsettled. As Wells puts it, *The Blair Witch Project* has recovered " 'suggestion' and 'allusion' in the horror film, and with them the idea that the most persuasive horror is the one suggested in the mind of the viewer, rather than that which is explicitly expressed on the screen" (2000: 108-109).

Interest in *The Blair Witch Project* was piqued before its release by the airing of a promotional short, *Curse of the Blair Witch,* on the Sci-Fi channel and by the posting of a Web site, <www.blairwitch.com>, both of which presented the legend and the three filmmakers' experiences as being real rather than Myrick and Sánchez's creation. The Web site offers a historical timeline of events, beginning in 1785 with several children accusing one Elly Kedward of extracting blood from them. Kedward was banished from the township of Blair, after which her accusers and half of the township's children mysteriously disappeared. A precise list of happenings over the centuries has an air of truth about it, such as an 1809 book titled *The Blair Witch Cult* and a hermit confessing in 1941 to having murdered and disemboweled children to appease a woman ghost. The site builds hype around the recovered footage by noting that the authorities kept it as evidence until 1997 (the students disappeared in 1994); what viewers of *The Blair Witch Project* will be seeing are those tapes, newly released to the students' parents and made into the movie by Haxan Films, a small production company. Links to pictures of Josh's abandoned car, Heather's journal, and select stills from the "recovered" film add credence to *The Blair Witch Project*'s reality.

Viewers were thus baited and eagerly anticipating the movie's release, and most were extremely scared by the overall experience: the hand-held camerawork, the eerie sounds heard from afar in the woods, the panic and terror expressed by the actors, the abrupt ending. It remains to be seen, but Myrick and Sánchez may have created what will become both a cult classic and a noteworthy artistic achievement, akin to Romero's *Night of the Living Dead.* (A sequel, *Book of Shadows: Blair Witch 2* [2000], directed by Joe Berlinger, lapses into standard horror film technique and was so poorly received that, hopefully, no further attempts to exploit the success of the first, truly original film will be forthcoming.)

Recently Darren Aronofsky, the maker of *Pi* (1998) and *Requiem for a Dream* (2000), has become bankable without yielding any of his artistic credibility. The attention that his first film (which was made for about $60,000) attracted gained him $5 million in financing for his second. *Pi* shakes with image jitters. In telling the story of a genius mathematician, Maximillian Cohen (Sean Gullette), Aronofsky constantly keeps viewers off balance and wondering what is real and what are Cohen's hallucinations. Having looked into the sun as a child, Cohen suffers headaches so severe that they cause nosebleeds, blood being a steadily repeated image that leads first to his seeing blood drip from the hand of a man on the subway platform that could be himself (viewers never fully see the man's face) and ultimately to his driving the electric drill he has been using on his computer equipment into his skull—a remark on the brain as computer. That act had also been foreshadowed by Cohen's poking at a brain he discovered in the subway while pursuing the mysterious bleeding man.

Aronofsky uses insects more subtly than the surrealists, from the ant that might have contributed to Cohen's computer crashing (the scene is far more than a play on a "bug" in a computer system) to the ants crawling on the brain in his bathroom sink after he drills into his own. The ants swarming out of a hole in a man's hand in *Un Chien Andalou*, however calmly the characters in the film take them, strike viewers as repulsive. The ants in *Pi* appear in lesser number; just one wanders around the inside of Cohen's computer, eluding him as he picks among the elements trying to determine what went wrong with the machine and, in turn, what went wrong in his numerical calculations. One normally expects to find cockroaches as the nasty insect featured in a city apartment, so Aronofsky's choice of ants deliberately avoids an immediate repulsive reaction in viewers and leads instead to their contemplation of the more insidious horror when they see the ants on the brain in the sink. Cohen's obsession with his mathematical calculation is brilliantly symbolized by the ants, the one in the computer's "brain" correlating to the several crawling about Cohen's brain, represented by the brain in the sink. Drilling into his own brain has exorcised the ceaseless agonizing; the "ants" have been removed from his mind. Blood and ants notwithstanding, probably the purest convention Aronofsky borrows from the horror genre is that of a locked and bolted door rattling violently as someone or something tries to assail Cohen in his apartment, representing both the groups who will stalk him and his own incipient madness breaking through.

Cohen survives his self-inflicted injury, freed of the torment of mathematics, and seems somewhat tranquil at the end of the film—at least the headaches and hallucinations have stopped. Aronofsky manages to interweave this tale of personal torment with an elaborate conspiracy theory involving a group of cabala scholars who want Cohen's assistance in cracking a code in the Torah that will enable them to speak God's name numerically and a group who wants to profit from Cohen's ability to predict the stock market.

Requiem for a Dream, an even more complex narrative, is a disturbing look at addiction, combining elements of horror with a traditional topic of exploitation movies. Sara Goldfarb (Ellen Burstyn) is a widow whose addiction to a television self-help game show, *The Tappy Tibbons Show,* leads to her addiction to amphetamines in the legal form of "diet pills." She believes a scam telephone call that makes her think she could appear on the show and wants to lose fifty pounds to once again fit into a red dress that represents memories of her most beautiful and happy self. Sara's son Harry (Jared Leto) is a heroin addict, as are Harry's friend Tyrone (Marlon Wayans) and girlfriend Marion (Jennifer Connelly). These four central characters have dreams of success and happiness, and Aronofsky lets viewers watch them disintegrate as drug abuse destroys the minds and bodies of each, which is the true horror of the film.

Aronofsky effectively repeats a montage of the shooting up, best described by *Orlando Weekly* movie reviewer Ian Grey (2000) as "a frenzied montage of micro-close-ups of fluids bubbling through tubes, their eyes dilating in time-lapse photography, leading to still shots of the users laid out like members of the living dead." The interesting camera work used in *Pi* continues here, with both horizontal and vertical split screens, overexposure, fast-motion photography, and even an attachment of a camera to a bungee cord to gain the proper effect for Harry's hallucination of falling. Aronofsky's cutting especially shows both the connections and divisions among the characters, most harrowingly in the closing fifteen minutes or so of the film. He is able to build incredible tension through pacing and cutting. *Requiem for a Dream* has over 2,000 cuts, whereas the average film contains 600 to 700 (Internet Movie Database, 2003).

Aronofsky may be dealing with an exploitation film topic, but the way he involves viewers with the characters evokes a feeling of compassion that lessens its sensational aspects. The last shot of the characters is of each of them curled in a fetal position, reduced to that state by an onslaught of experiences that are the staple not only of horror films, but of real life as well: electroshock therapy, amputation, being forced to swallow something against one's will.

Aronofsky cowrote the screenplay for *Requiem for a Dream* with Hubert Selby Jr., author of the 1978 novel of the same name. His investment in his scripts, coupled with his filming techniques, are positive indications of Aronofsky's bringing important elements of avant-garde and horror films to mainstream cinema. When the Motion Picture Association of America refused to repeal its NC-17 rating of *Requiem for a Dream,* Artisan Entertainments (which had distributed *The Blair Witch Project*) stood behind the work and released the film unrated. As movies whose budgets exceed that of vital government agencies such as the Environmental Protection Agency continue to fall flat, perhaps more studios will realize that, often, low budgets and tight schedules lead to innovation—and even art.

Chapter 2

"And I Brought You Nightmares": The Play of Horror in Hitchcock's Films

Although Alfred Hitchcock is considered the "master of suspense" and worked hard at conveying that image, he is actually a covert master of horror. Certain recurring themes and techniques place his films squarely in the horror genre, even making them closer to true horror than the self-proclaimed horror films of his time. Like all popular genres, both horror and suspense traditionally serve to entertain. A key difference lies in the intensity of that entertainment. Both genres manipulate viewers' emotions—specifically fear—but do so in different ways. Suspense intends to titillate, to quicken the pulse through intrigue and threat of imminent danger. Horror is the dark cousin, the relation suspense tries to keep in the basement. It exploits taboos and unmentionable desires, most especially those involving sadomasochistic impulses. Hitchcock's painstaking control of his scripts in preparation and execution is legendary. Less often commented on are the underlying emotions that fueled his inspiration and the way they surface in his movies. Stories are legion of his cruel treatment of actors and others in the industry—but what about the audience?

In general, the horror genre is associated with supernatural occurrences, but much of the finest horror—in literature or film—deals with psychological terror. Think of Robert Louis Stevenson's works (*Dr. Jekyll and Mr. Hyde, The Body Snatcher),* Mary Shelley's *Frankenstein,* or the tales of Edgar Allan Poe. During the time Hitchcock was working, most of the films labeled "horror" were really closer to the Gothic and fantasy/science fiction genres: the Frankenstein movies, the paranoiac melodramas such as *Invasion of the Body Snatchers* (1956). Granted, such examples show how fluid are the boundaries among these popular genres. But Hitchcock, at his darkest, was exposing elements and situations that virtually no other mainstream director was dealing with at the time: incest, random cruelty, systematic destruction of an individual, coercion into unspeakable acts, desecration of innocence, the irretrievability of the pathological consciousness. In this respect Hitchcock is similar to Poe, whose layering of texts allowed him to write about exactly these issues while gaining publication in major newspapers and magazines. Indeed, Hitchcock wrote a fascinating essay pondering his debt to Poe, titled "Why I Am Afraid of the Dark" (1995), in which he notes the following:

> I try to put into my films what Poe put in his stories: a perfectly unbelievable story recounted to readers with such a hallucinatory logic that one has the impression that this same story can happen to you tomorrow. And that's the rule of the game if one wants the reader or the spectator to subconsciously substitute himself for the hero, because, in truth, people are only interested in themselves or in stories which could affect them. (143)

These remarks get at a key technique of suspense in Hitchcock's films, one that permits the psychological themes to escalate into true horror: viewers' closeness to or distance from the characters in the films. In *Hitchcock: Suspense, Humour and Tone,* Susan Smith (2000) identifies three kinds of suspense at interplay in Hitchcock's films: *vicarious suspense,* the kind of emotion felt for Stevie, the young boy in *Sabotage* (1936) whom the traitor Verloc sends across town with a bomb; *shared suspense,* in which viewers fear *with,* not just *for,* a character, heightening their identification with that character; and *direct suspense,* when viewers' fears are for *themselves,* such as in the shower scene in *Psycho,* when Marion steps back and it is as if the viewer is about to be attacked. Of course, Hitchcock used these types of suspense in various combinations. Smith offers the example of *Frenzy* (1972), "where the disturbing impact of sharing Brenda Blaney's consciousness during the rape and murder scene fuels the intensity of the vicarious suspense later on when [the villain] Rusk invites Babs back to his apartment" (Smith, 2000: 21).

Because of such elements, Smith argues that *Psycho* "travels much further along the suspense scale [than Hitchcock's other films] by going beyond fear to give us horror" (2000: 26). As she explains it, "The sudden intrusion of moments of horror, following the prolonged build-up of acute tension . . . , serves to create a rhetorical rhythm deep within the film's textual structures. The overall effect of this is to convey a sense of anarchic, uncontainable forces capable of erupting at any time" (2000: 27). All Smith is saying is perceptive, but *Psycho* is not the only Hitchcock film to veer into horror. In fact, he repeatedly used the suspense form as a smokescreen through which he could introduce elements that might otherwise have been too extreme and unacceptable to both his employers and the general public.

In his most powerful films, Hitchcock builds, or simply leaps, from an atmosphere of climactic tension to the nightmare realm. He understood that sometimes entertainment is brutal. For instance, *Spellbound* (1945), a relatively sedate thriller, climaxes with a flashback of the protagonist accidentally pushing his brother onto the spikes of a wrought-iron railing; the scene could easily fit into a Stephen King novel. (In reference to the previous chapter's discussion of surrealism and horror, Hitchcock obtained the surrealistic effect he wanted for *Spellbound*'s dream sequences by having Salvador Dalí create them [Harris and Lasky, 1993: 122].) In *Shadow of a Doubt* (1943), Uncle Charlie tries to asphyxiate his niece by locking her in a garage with a running car. In *Sabotage,* viewers are confronted by the explosion on the bus. Certainly, the carousel sequence in *Strangers on a Train* (1951) is a perfect example, so much so that both Hitchcock and François Truffaut felt it went too far. Typically, here the real horror is implied. For all the power of what is on film, what truly appalls is the unwitnessed wounding, crippling, and killing of the children on the carousel. That Hitchcock could get away with the scene at all testifies to his cunning skill at understatement, even in one of his most breathtaking sequences.

Indeed, this corruption or slaughter of the innocent is one of those themes Hitchcock exploited to a point beyond simple entertainment. In *Sabotage,* the simple boy Stevie (Desmond Tester) is used as a carrier by his sister's husband Verloc (Oscar Homolka), a saboteur who plans to blow up a part of Piccadilly Circus. Tensely, viewers watch the predetermined time of the explosion grow nearer as Stevie transports the film case containing the bomb across town. Hitchcock does the unthinkable. Whereas viewers would hope for their tension to be relieved in Stevie's life being spared, Hitchcock blows him up— along with a busload of people and a puppy. This is another instance in which Hitchcock claimed to feel that he went too far, but he said that about several movies which were criticized for alienating the popular audience. Further, Stevie's death leads to the corruption of his sister, Sylvia (Sylvia Sidney), when she realizes what Verloc has done and is driven to vengeful murder. Hitchcock films a quiet dining room scene in which Sylvia is carving meat; her emotions build until she plunges the knife into her husband.

Writing about *The Birds* (1963), William Paul proposes,

> There is nothing more nefarious than taking advantage of a child because a child presents a kind of double vulnerability. Not only are children less capable of defending against assault. Lacking more fully developed powers of ratiocination, they are less able to explore and determine possible reasons for the seemingly un-motivated assault, reasons that might offer a way of dealing with it. (1994: 256)

There is no reason for the assaults the birds make on humans in *The Birds,* which just adds to the horror. Viewers watch over Melanie's (Tippi Hedren's) shoulders as crows assemble on the playground equipment outside of a small schoolhouse, within which children are singing. When Melanie becomes aware of the mass of birds, she warns the schoolteacher, Annie (Suzanne Pleshette), and all race for their lives down the hill into town. The children are terrorized, and Hitchcock focuses on one who is attacked and who falls to the ground, breaking her eyeglasses. Not only has she been physically hurt by the birds, but she has to suffer the additional panic brought about by being unable to see clearly.

Nastier still is the abuse that Hitchcock studies in *Marnie* (1964). As a child, Marnie (Tippi Hedren) has to endure various men visiting her home to see her mother, Bernice (Louise Latham), who is a pros-titute. When one of them, an unnamed sailor (Bruce Dern), starts coming on to Marnie and then beats Bernice when she intervenes, Marnie kills him. This repressed childhood event causes Marnie to be a sexually frigid adult who steals money from her employers and moves from city to city, creating new identities for herself. One boss, Mark Rutland (Sean Connery), falls in love with Marnie and marries her, then nearly rapes her on their honeymoon, which pushes Marnie to attempt suicide. Ultimately Marnie's memory is recovered, and viewers vicariously share in her childhood trauma.

Desecration of innocence, this time paired with suggestions of in-cest, are integral parts of the plot of *Shadow of a Doubt.* Uncle Charlie (Joseph Cotten), widow murderer, corrupts his niece's worldview, and the development from insinuation to threat underscores the degradation. Cotten plays the slimiest and most endearing killer in all of Hitchcock's movies; the menace and disorientation the niece increasingly senses lies in the dialogue and Cotten's representation of the character. The ties between uncle and niece are nearly telepathic. "We're sort of like twins," young Charlie (Teresa Wright) says at one point. Not knowing her uncle has already sent word that he is coming for a visit, Charlie, bored with the routine of her home life—which includes, amusingly enough, her father Joe (Henry Travers) and his friend Herb (Hume Cronyn) trying to think up the perfect way to murder each other—declares, "I know a wonderful person who will come shake us all up." And Uncle Charlie starts doing just that almost immediately. Family photographs from some fifty years previous cause the uncle to observe, "Everybody was sweet and pretty then, Charlie. The whole world. A wonderful world. Not like the world today." Trying to defend her uncle's privacy from detectives posing as reporters who want to do a piece on "an average kind of family," she asks them, "Are you trying to tell me I shouldn't think he's so wonderful?" She is answered with Uncle Charlie's demanding the film after they take his photograph. Keeping company with one of the reporters, Charlie is dismayed to learn that he is a detective, and further upset at being made to suspect her uncle of murder. Then Uncle Charlie's speech about widows slaps her in the face: "Horrible, faded, fat . . . What do they do, these useless women? Drinking their money, eating their money, smelling of money . . . horrible."

Her disillusionment and contamination by her uncle's worldview reaches its height (or nadir) in a scene at the Til Two bar, where Hitchcock brings the signs, signifiers, and nightmares to a crescendo. When Charlie storms out of the house following one of her father's morbid, murder-related after-dinner conversations, Uncle Charlie chases her and, twisting her arm painfully, drags her into the seedy establishment. Seated in a booth, he wheedles her with remarks such as, "We're old friends, Charlie. More than that. We're like twins; you said so yourself." He asks pointed questions about the detective she has been talking to, referring to him as "that boy" with the inflection of a jealous lover. As he speaks he chokes a paper napkin, then, noticing Charlie watching him, lowers his hands beneath the table. This charming tête-à-tête culminates in one of the most nihilistic and disturbing speeches in all of cinema:

> "You think you know something, don't you? You think you're the clever little girl who knows something. There's so much you don't know. So much. What do you know, really? You're just an ordinary little girl living in an ordinary little town. You wake up every morning of your life and you know perfectly well that there's nothing in the world to trouble you. You go through your ordinary little day and at night you sleep your untroubled, ordinary little sleep filled with peaceful stupid dreams. And I brought you nightmares. . . . You live in a dream, you're a sleepwalker, blind! How do you know what the world is like? Do you know the world is a foul sty? Do you know if you ripped the fronts off houses you'd find swine? The world's a hell! What does it matter what happens in it?"

"The same blood flows through our veins," the uncle says, and Hitchcock tops off the film by making that statement horrendously true. Uncle Charlie tries to throw his niece off of a moving train and, in defending herself, young Charlie becomes the reason *he* falls off the train. In essence, she has become a murderer too: further desecration of her innocence and the culmination of what has been a systematic destruction of her character at the hand of her uncle.

The suggestions of incest grow stronger as *Shadow of a Doubt* progresses. When telephoning his sister to announce his upcoming visit, Charlie tells her, "And a kiss for little Charlie, from her Uncle Charlie," on the surface an innocent enough greeting. But the girl's bedroom becomes his guest room; as he gazes at her high school graduation picture, he places a rose in his lapel hole, an action Hitchcock comments on with a bit of sinister music. Charlie beams when her friends see her around town with her uncle, and at her father's bank, where Uncle Charlie is depositing his ill-gotten gains, he fondles his niece's hand more like a beau than an uncle. When she pounces on the newspaper pages about the Merry Widow Murderer that he tries to hide, he grabs her wrist *hard,* and the two struggle as battling lovers do in dozens of films. Incidentally, this scene takes place in the bedroom.

"Deviant" sex is a hallmark of film noir, from *The Big Sleep* (1946) to *White Heat* (1949) to *The Naked Kiss* (1964). But all those films brought that subject in tangentially, as a kind of quasi-sociological ingredient. Hitchcock, on the other hand, employed fetishism as a link between eroticism and terror—most famously in his explorations of voyeurism, but as frequently in other manifestations. For instance, the psychiatrist at the end of *Psycho* explains what Norman Bates (Anthony Perkins) did to his mother and how his wearing her clothes was not a form of sexual expression, but he leaves unmentioned the crucial factor of the necrophiliac fetishization of his mother's corpse. First Norman killed his mother and her lover (preserving Mother's body), then felt driven to murder sexually enticing and threatening women such as Marion (Janet Leigh). This is far afield of James Cagney's "Top of the world, Ma!" and much closer to the pre-Freudian world of Matthew Lewis' *The Monk* or Poe's "Ligeia."

Most revealing, though, is Hitchcock's fascination with strangulation, a central part of *Shadow of a Doubt* as well as of *The Lodger* (1927), *Rope* (1948), *Dial "M" for Murder* (1954), *Strangers on a Train,* and *Frenzy.* It is even alluded to in *Sabotage:* the film case Stevie carries is for Bartholomew the Strangler. Death by lack of oxygen is one of the most primal fears, and when people are not being strangled in Hitchcock's movies they often suffer some similar peril of asphyxiation, as when young Charlie nearly dies from carbon monoxide poisoning in *Shadow of a Doubt,* or when a Communist agent in *Topaz* (1969) finally succumbs, after an excruciatingly protracted murder attempt, by having his head shoved into an unlit gas oven. Even private detective Arbogast's death in *Psycho* implies strangulation: obviously, he died from having his neck broken during his fall down the stairs. Strangulation is the most simple, primitive form of murder; it is also the most intimate. In that sense the killer is both completely alienated from humanity and completely engaged with it.

Certainly the most sexually charged strangulation scene is in *Strangers on a Train.* The killer Bruno Anthony (Robert Walker) trails the cheating wife, Miriam Haines (Laura Elliott), at a carnival she is attending with not one, but two dates. She seems to find the dark-suited Bruno more interesting than her college-boy escorts, licking an ice cream cone seductively as she glances at him, looking back for him when the trio stops at a game, and exchanging smiles with him as he joins in singing "The Band Played On" when all four get on a carousel. He stalks them through the Tunnel of Love and across the lake to Magic Isle, riding in a boat aptly named after the god of the underworld, Pluto. On the island meant to be a Lovers' Lane, Bruno catches Miriam alone when she flirtingly runs away from her two paramours. As he attacks her, her eyeglasses fall to the ground, and the murder is shown reflected in the lenses. In his classic study on Hitchcock, *Hitchcock's Films Revisited,* Robin Wood points out the network of symbolism that runs through this sequence: "The lens itself recalls lake and tunnel and is a further sexual symbol. The shot is one of the cinema's most powerful images of perverted sexuality, the murder a sexual culmination for both killer and victim" (1960: 90). Beyond that, we would emphasize the relation of intimacy and destruction, as Miriam's mouth opens in an expression reminiscent of the throes of passion—an association Hitchcock would make explicit to the point of pornography in the movie *Frenzy*—and, as he strangles her, Bruno gradually lays Miriam's body down the way a tender lover might. A later scene in *Strangers on a Train* underscores the relation between sex and strangulation, when Bruno is playfully demonstrating a proper strangling on a society matron at a soiree. Over her shoulder he notices the eyeglasses on Barbara Morton (Pat Hitchcock) and, hearing the carnival music and slipping into a trance, squeezes tighter and tighter until he abruptly faints, which seems an allusion to an old-fashioned Victorian swoon of sexual repression.

Although doubling is a favorite motif of Patricia Highsmith, whose 1950 novel serves as the basis for the film, Hitchcock is often drawn to it as well, and here he fairly revels in it. His cameo appearance in *Strangers on a Train* comes as Guy Haines (Farley Granger) disembarks from a train: Hitchcock struggles to board while carrying a double bass in its instrument case. Bruno orders scotch and water—"A pair, doubles!"—on the train for himself and Guy when they first meet, and the two men are linked from there on. Part of Bruno's function is to represent "the destructive, subversive urges that exist, though suppressed, in everybody: he is an extension, an embodiment, of desires already existing in Guy" (Wood, 1960: 87-88). This is underscored by the suggestion of a latent homosexual relationship between Bruno and Guy, with some stereotypical gay behavior being attributed to Bruno. Shaking hands when they meet, Bruno places both of his hands over Guy's one; he is a dandy who fancies winged-tip shoes and silk robes; his mother gives him manicures; and at one point he chastizes Guy for not telephoning him, the way a jilted lover would. He invites Guy to his train compartment for a secluded lunch, which is where he lays out his elaborate plan.

Part of the horror of this film is how Guy is drawn inexorably into Bruno's madman "crisscross" scheme of swapping murders. "I'm your friend; I'll do anything for you," Bruno declares, and he expects the same in return. Guy wants to be free of his wife, who is pregnant with another man's child, so that he can marry the woman he loves, and Bruno proposes that he kill Miriam and that Guy kill Bruno's hated father to eliminate the motives. Guy does not really think Bruno is serious about this, but he unwittingly agrees to it by placating Bruno with, "Sure, we talk the same language. . . . Sure, all your ideas are okay," as he tries to get out of Bruno's compartment. When Guy is angered over Miriam's reneging on the divorce because of his monetary success in tennis tournaments and his interest in Ann Morton (Ruth Roman), he says to Ann, "I'd like to break her useless neck!" After doing just that, Bruno lurks in the shadows across from Guy's row home, gives Guy Miriam's glasses, and informs him he is an accessory to murder. When a police car pulls up, Guy steps back into the shadows with Bruno, lamenting, "You've got me acting like a criminal!"

Doubles appear again when Guy is kept under observation by a detective, while Bruno turns up everywhere from the bleachers at a tennis match to a soiree at the Mortons' to the steps of the Thomas Jefferson Memorial—this last being a nice touch, since the quotation on its inside rotunda reads, "I have sworn upon the altar of God eternal hostility against every form of tyranny over the mind of man." The two men's identities come the closest to being conflated in the final carousel scene. Bruno has returned to the carnival to plant Guy's lighter on Magic Isle as incriminating evidence. Guy spots Bruno in the crowd and runs after him; two policemen are chasing Guy, convinced he is the murderer; a carnival worker who recognized Bruno as being on the scene the night of the murder is leading another pair of police after *him;* and when Bruno and Guy jump aboard the carousel, the police shoot at Guy but kill the carousel operator. Thence begins one of the most tense and horrifying scenes in Hitchcock's entire body of work, as the carousel achieves a deadly speed and the two men struggle with each other under the descending and ascending hooves of the wooden horses. A carny crawls beneath the ride and throws a lever that brings the carousel to a screeching halt. The screams and traumatized faces of the mothers in the crowd are Hitchcock's way of conveying the maimed and dead riders. Except, of course, Guy and, for just long enough to exonerate him, Bruno.

Hitchcock suggests the intimacy of strangulation in more subtle ways, too. Most intriguingly, in *Shadow of a Doubt* Uncle Charlie gives his niece a ring taken from one of his victims. Hitchcock may be the first artist to have ever noted a connection between strangulation and betrothal as signified by a ring. After all, the one that the uncle slips onto Charlie's finger comes from a woman he married and then choked to death. Such an association does not seem so far-fetched when one recalls that in the early film *The Lodger,* the detective, Joe (Malcolm Keen), comments, "When I've put a rope around the Avenger's neck, I'll put a ring round Daisy's finger" (cited in Barr, 1999: 33). That sentiment in turn calls to mind a remark made by the waitress in the bar scene in *Shadow of a Doubt.* Seeing the ring Uncle Charlie gave his niece, the woman says wistfully, "I'd just die for a ring like that."

Hitchcock is noted for attaching great significance to small items such as rings and cigarette lighters. The piece of jewelry that trips up the strangler in *Frenzy* is a tie pin, since he uses his tie as a murder weapon. It is worth noting that the opening predicament of a stran-gled woman's body turning up in a river had been used by Hitchcock before, in a film revealingly titled, given Hitchcock's penchant for the desecration of youth, *Young and Innocent* (1937) in its British release and *The Girl Was Young* (1937) in its American release. *Frenzy*'s plot relies on mistaken identity, with Richard Blaney (Jon Finch) being sought for the murder of his ex-wife Brenda (Barbara Leigh-Hunt), whereas the real killer is Bob Rusk (Barry Foster). Rusk is a serial rapist-murderer who strangles Brenda because her matchmaking agency has too normal a clientele to provide him with the kind of women who will "submit" to the "peculiarities" that appeal to him, as Brenda explains to the misogynist. As mentioned, Brenda's mouth in death is wide open, but her tongue lolls out grotesquely, making the image a pornographic jointure of sexuality and morbidity. Although Rusk is assumed to be "governed by the pleasure principle" and therefore "particularly dangerous" when his desire is frustrated, more to the point is a Scotland Yard detective's observation, "In the latter stage of the disease, it's the strangling, not the sex, that brings them out."

Likewise, one character in *Frenzy* surmises, "The man who's killing these women is a criminal, sexual, psychopath. And the legal profession has never really known how to treat them. I suppose you could call them social misfits." Hitchcock made "social misfits" the central characters of numerous films as he studied the irretrievability of the pathological consciousness. Sometimes there is a hint of the source of the character's pathology, such as Uncle Charlie in *Shadow of a Doubt* having been hit by a car when he was a boy and sustaining a skull fracture; or Bruno's inheriting a mental instability that appears in a more benign form in his dotty mother. But while the psychiatrist at the end of *Psycho* allows that Norman's murdering his mother and her lover is what induced his schizophrenia, multiple personality, and homicidal tendencies, he does not go into why Norman killed his mother in the first place. It is more disturbing to watch Uncle Charlie's methodical desecration of his niece's innocence and more frightening to follow Rusk on his course of rape and murder than to ruminate on what causes such behavior.

Likewise, while guilt and a fear of heights contribute to and explain the protagonist's actions in *Vertigo* (1958), his necrophilia is rather unsettling. John "Scottie" Ferguson (James Stewart) falls in love with a woman named Madeleine whom he saves from drowning herself, a woman he believes is the wife of his friend, Gavin Elster (Tom Helmore). Madeleine seems obsessed with an ancestor who had committed suicide. Scottie suffers intense guilt when Madeleine falls to her death from the tower of the Mission at San Juan Batista; his vertigo had prevented his climbing the tower with her. When he meets Judy Barton (Kim Novak), who bears a striking resemblance to the dead Madeleine (also played by Novak), he tries to make her into Madeleine by having her dress similarly and wear her hair in the same style. It turns out that Elster is having an affair with Judy and had her pose as his wife in order to use Scottie as an eyewitness to her "accidental" death, for the woman who had plummeted from the tower was the real, murdered Madeleine. Scottie forces Judy to return to the mission tower to confess this, and Hitchcock conveys Scottie's acrophobia with dizzying camerawork, achieved by zooming forward while tracking backward (Harris and Lasky, 1993). A nun startles the couple, and Judy plunges to her death. Scottie's obsessive desire for a dead woman is actually the cause of her demise, yet Hitchcock makes viewers completely empathetic to this protagonist, not least because he makes them share his vertiginous perspective. Geoffrey O'Brien has noted that Hitchcock breaks the Hollywood formula of love/loss/love and, with great significance, uses the structure of "fatal fall/orgasmic embrace/fatal fall/orgasmic embrace/fatal fall" (2002: 136).

Fear of heights and a fear of falling are widely shared phobias, and waiting to see whether a character on screen plummets makes for good suspense, but Hitchcock took this to extremes by putting the viewer in the position of the imperiled through such camerawork as that employed in *Vertigo*. He made the viewer feel the fear of falling in *Young and Innocent, Saboteur* (1942), and *North by Northwest* (1959). On a smaller scale, he inserted a short fall out of a window in *Rear Window* (1954), the lethal tumble down the stairs in *Psycho*, and the potential fall down a flight of exterior stairs in *Shadow of a Doubt*, where Uncle Charlie deliberately breaks a step in order to trip up his niece.

Arguments have gone back and forth over the level of subversion in Hitchcock's films. (Those who cannot sense any subversion are his perfect audience.) On a purely formal level, his greatest subversion lies not only in bringing both horror and humor into what are ostensibly suspense films but also in combining these elements in such a way that they prove integral, even imperative, to the story. Take, for example, the scene that leads to the appalling carousel massacre in *Strangers on a Train*. It is staged like a John Ford showdown, and played for both laughs and tension, with Pat Hitchcock at her most charming and beguiling when distracting a detective from following Guy by spilling face powder all over his trousers. The song playing as Bruno gets in line for the boat ride to Magic Isle to plant Guy's lighter is "Ain't We Got Fun?" Humor appears in *Psycho* when Norman becomes disconcerted at how Marion's car stops sinking and throws nervous, birdlike looks behind him to see if anyone is watching. It is sprinkled into various conversations which the first-time viewer of that film would recognize as funny, but rewatching lets viewers in on the economy of taxidermy as a hobby; Marion's unwitting quip that "A man should have a hobby"; Norman's observation that "a boy's best friend is his mother"; and that, despite his mother's "illness," "Why, she's as harmless as one of those stuffed birds."

Hitchcock has remarked that "'suspense' doesn't have any value if it's not balanced by humor" (1995: 144), and his films certainly bear this out. Film critic Anthony Lane observes, "as with any good Hitchcock, from 'The Lodger' onward, material that should leave you humbled and wrecked sends you out on a mystified high. Hitchcock was once asked why he had never made a comedy. 'But every film I make *is* a comedy,' he replied" (1999: 85). Horror, as can be seen in everything from the original Bela Lugosi *Dracula* (1931) movie to the corrosive wit of David Cronenberg, is inextricably connected to humor, and no director has understood this better than Hitchcock. A sensibility that could conceive of a sluttish music store clerk, who looks like a stereotypical librarian, being shown strangled in the reflection of her eyeglass lenses as a carnival version of "The Band Played On" sounds in the background, or who could turn an invitation to "Nothing special, just sandwiches and milk" into the pathetic come-on of a deranged killer, is one that thoroughly comprehends the implicit madness lying beneath our world of jocular hostility. *Shadow of a Doubt* testifies to this, with Hitchcock's paralleling the downward spiral of both Charlies with Herb and Joe's obsessive hypothetical murdering of each other. Jokingly he thrusts the titles of their favorite reading material before viewers—*UNSOLVED CRIMES, CRIME MAGAZINE*—just as he presents newspaper headlines about Uncle Charlie's crimes: "Where Is the Merry Widow Murderer?" No wonder young Charlie snaps when the dinner table chat turns once again to her "father's way of relaxing": "Can't we have a little peace and quiet around here without dragging in poison all the time?" she rails.

Much like Franz Kafka or, more to the point, Poe, two other masters who knew the value of humor when delving into the darker aspects of human nature, Hitchcock focused obsessively on his obsessions. All three artists dealt with a limited range of experience and emotion, to the point of unhealthiness, even morbidity. And while one would not want to live in the worlds they created (any more than they wanted to), one cannot dismiss their contributions to the larger culture. It is a sad fact of humanity that innocence gets destroyed; that people can be cruel, can kill; that families have their dark, dirty secrets. Alfred Hitchcock not only brought us nightmares; he helps us to live with the nightmares we cannot avoid. That is the mark of a master—not of suspense, but of horror.

Chapter 3

Horror, Humor, Poetry:
Sam Raimi's *Evil Dead* Trilogy

In making films, Sam Raimi transformed his chosen genre: the inane B-movie drive-in horror flick. Out of a mixture of love for low-budget horror films with a marked skepticism for their aesthetic worth and a desire to both parody and elevate them, he shaped three unique creations—*The Evil Dead* (1981), *Evil Dead II: Dead by Dawn* (1987), and *Army of Darkness* (1993)—using a blend of gore and camp that mocks its own excesses. Yet as gory or campy as any of these movies become, they always contain extended passages of poetic beauty. This threefold quality—horror, humor, poetry—tends to be both confusing and exhilarating and sets Raimi's horror films apart from more typical and simplistic offerings, ranging from Herschell Gordon Lewis' original gore-fests to Wes Craven's later splatter-deconstructions.

Given the inherently bizarre qualities of the horror genre—hovering apparitions; stumbling monsters, mummies, and zombies; spring-latched revolving bookcases; and so forth—surprisingly few horror films indulge in self-consciously humorous and absurd scenes. There are exceptions, certainly: the spin-offs from EC Comics' *Tales from the Crypt,* for instance, or many of Roger Corman's movies. But the majority tend to be quite humorless, even if they are unintentionally comic. In the latter category, the *Friday the 13th* series comes to mind, along with more "high-minded" vehicles such as James Whale's *Frankenstein* (1931) or Tod Browning's *Dracula* (1931), or, for that matter, the later Hammer Films' versions based on these same characters. Regardless, no films have ever played with horror conventions as anticly as the *Evil Dead* trilogy.

Raimi claims that at the outset of his career, as a viewer, he did not like horror films. He and his friends from high school and college made them because they believed horror films would be lucrative. Things quickly changed, as Raimi explained in an interview with Rebecca Mead. He started studying horror films and recognized the artistry that went into making them, and found the process intriguing. Observing the effect of suspense on audiences, he began wondering how to bring viewers to a certain level and keep them there. Should a suspenseful scene be ended by scaring the audience, letting them down gently, or exhilirating them, Raimi pondered, equating making a horror film with creating a piece of music, and describing watching them as viewing a musical composition (Mead, 1998). Raimi is indeed a composer of visual music. The *Evil Dead* films demonstrate that he knows how long to sustain a high note, when to punctuate a scene with staccato action, when to hush down to dimuendo. And there is an underlying, repeating theme in terms of images and content that runs through the three movies: the *Necronomicon* and its attendant philosophy, as proposed by H. P. Lovecraft.

The *Necronomicon* is a fictional legend conjured up in the work of Lovecraft and articulated most fully in his 1927 essay titled "History of the *Necronomicon*." Lovecraft claims that the book was written by "a mad poet of Sanaa, in Yemen," one Abdul Alhazred, around A.D. 700 (1927: 1). Interestingly, given the action in the *Evil Dead* films, Alhazred reputedly met his demise when he was "seized by an invisible monster in broad daylight and devoured horribly before a large number of fright-frozen witnesses" (Lovecraft, 1927: 1). In the first two *Evil Dead* movies, the book is referred to as *Noturum de Monto,* but it is clearly meant to be the *Necronomicon*. In the first film it is described as being bound in human flesh and inked in human blood. The archaeologist's voice on the tape says it contains Sumerian burial practices and funerary incantations and has the power to recall demons that "may lie dormant but are never truly dead"; once evoked, they are "given license to possess the living." In the second movie, the book is a passageway to the evil world beyond and was written "when the seas ran red with blood"; it was this blood that was used to inscribe the pages. In the third movie, if the book falls into the hands of the dead, all humanity will be consumed with evil. The *Necronomicon,* then, serves as the vehicle for the horrific in each of the *Evil Dead* films.

The first two *Evil Dead* movies use the similar situation of a remote cabin in the woods. In *The Evil Dead,* five friends from Michigan State stay there: Ash (Bruce Campbell), the protagonist in all three films, and his girlfriend Linda (Betsy Baker); Scotty (Hal Delrich) and his girlfriend Shelly (Sarah York); and Ash's sister, Cheryl (Ellen Sandweiss). Exploring the cabin, they find the *Necronomicon* in the basement and play a tape recording that invokes evil spirits. In *Evil Dead II,* just Ash and Linda (Denise Bixler) come to the cabin. They play a recording made by a professor of ancient history, Raymond Knowby (John Peaks), who had brought the *Necronomicon* to the cabin to translate it, unintentionally unleashing "a thing of evil that roams the forest and dark bowers of man's domain." He had to kill his wife, Henrietta, and bury her body in the basement because she had become host to a demon. Again, playing the tape invokes the spirits. Later in the movie, Knowby's daughter, Annie (Sarah Berry), and a local couple, Jake (Dan Hicks) and Bobbie Joe (Kassie Wesley), serving as her guides arrive, and soon become caught up in the action.

The setting changes for the final film in the trilogy. *Army of Darkness* is set in a mythomedieval land that figured into the ending of *Evil Dead II.* A Merlinesque figure known as Wiseman (Ian Abercrombie) agrees to send the lone Ash back to his own time if he retrieves the *Necronomicon* from a cemetery. The plot is a parody of the archetypal hero quest, such as *The Epic of Gilgamesh* or Arthurian legends, with Ash encountering various demons and dangerous situations as he works his way toward the cemetery.

From the beginning of the first *Evil Dead* movie Raimi exploits horror conventions at the same time he revels in their possibilities. Queasy camera angles give the tilting point of view of some evil force racing through the Tennessee woods. (Raimi attached a camera to a board to achieve the ground-level perspective [Mead, 1998].) Five young people are careering toward their vacation cabin in the middle of nowhere, planks giving way beneath them as they cross an old bridge posted with the sign "Dangerous Bridge. Cross at Your Own Risk." At the cabin, a porch swing is banging insistently against the wall, although there is no wind. When Scotty grabs a key from atop the lintel, the swinging abruptly stops. The group enters, fulfilling the most important of horror conventions: When everything in the world is telling you to run, you plod confidently straight into hell.

Sometimes Raimi likes to jolt viewers by brandishing conventions and then topping them with something truly horrifying. In *The Evil*

Dead a branch breaks the cabin window in Cheryl's bedroom, a thunderstorm churns up, a giant full moon floats in the sky—then the evil force in the woods roars "Join us!"—and Cheryl stupidly leaves the cabin. But no one could expect what happens next, even with the foreshadowing element of the branch coming through the window: Vines snake around Cheryl's limbs and neck, cut off her bathrobe, and drag her to the ground, where a hurtling branch—more like a shaft, really—rapes her. (A similar scene occurs in *Evil Dead II* when Bobbie Joe runs out of the cabin and vines grab her, rip her blouse, probe her mouth, muzzle her, then pull her across the ground at a fierce speed to slam her, lethally, into a tree.) Another unexpected invasion comes at the close of the film where Raimi has viewers thinking there will be a happy ending. Birds and a rosy dawn greet Ash as he staggers out of the cabin; light music plays on the soundtrack. Of course something is going to happen, but the visualized roar that starts in the woods behind the cabin, rushes through the building, and bursts out the front toward Ash's gaping mouth makes one laugh with surprise, perhaps because viewers realize the apparent sole survivor has ultimately lost the fight.

Raimi joyfully exploits the cheesiest of conventions, such as the voice-over at the start of *Evil Dead II* explaining the origin of the *Necronomicon* or a hackneyed moment later in the same film where Professor Knowby's ghost appears and advises his daughter and the others in a dramatic tone, "Recite the passages. Dispel the evil. Save my soul, and your own minds!" Raimi likes going one better than other writers and filmmakers, too. Echoing a scene in Shirley Jackson's 1959 novel *The Haunting of Hill House* and its movie version, *The Haunting* (1963), Bobbie Joe says, "Jake, you're holding my hand too tight." Jake replies, "Baby, I ain't holdin' your hand," and all look down to see a graphic addition to Jackson's idea: Ash's severed hand is gripping the girl's.

One of the key elements to the *Evil Dead* trilogy is the subjective treatment of space and perspective, representing interior states of being through cinematic terms. The idea has origins as much in literature as in the visual arts, especially Gothic literature. It is a form of phantasmagoria, of shifting perspectives reinforcing a central, if disintegrating, point of view. It has been employed cinematically in many ways, from the subtlety of Roman Polanski's *Repulsion* (1965) to the extravagance of Wes Craven's *The People Under the Stairs*

(1991). Raimi's vision falls somewhere in between, or beyond. In the first two *Evil Dead* movies, viewers see a tiny cabin in a huge forest, but the cabin expands almost endlessly once the characters are inside; the sizes of the rooms shift, and the box becomes a labyrinth. When characters are outside, the woods constrict claustrophobically around them. The basement is much too large for the size of the dwelling above it, a huge space with odd light sources and, despite the fact that it is cold outside, condensation dripping off of the pipes. In *The Evil Dead* Raimi uses the basement to create an extended poetic sequence that echoes the technique of Jean Cocteau as well as that of early surrealist films.

Ash goes to the basement for shotgun shells, and a cloth that appears to have been wrapped around a pipe to seal a leak falls apart; blood gushes onto Ash, blood oozes from electrical outlets, blood fills a light bulb. A gramophone and film projector start, and blood fills the lens of the latter, which is projecting its bloody images on Ash. Drip, drip goes the blood out of the pipe until there is a bloody river on the floor. Dripping blood in most horror films alerts a character to the location of a dead, mutilated body. Here, Raimi composes a scene that expands the use of blood into a truly haunting experience. Ash hears a montage of voices from the past, some positive and some negative, but recalling Scotty's command to "hit her, hit *it*" after Cheryl is demonized, he loads the shotgun and shoots the film projector. Light bulbs blow up on their own, the gramophone dies down, and Ash hears only the drip, drip of blood from the pipes. He wades through puddles of blood returning upstairs (viewers receive a moment of humorous relief if they notice the band aid can floating in the blood) and enters another surreal space. The clock is spinning its hands and camera shots go askew to indicate that the evil force is surrounding him: Viewers see Ash from a floor shot, an upside down shot, then one that flips around to show him from the front. After slamming the door to keep the force outside the cabin, Ash approaches the mirror and reaches out to his reflection, putting his hand into the glass as it becomes a liquid pool, Raimi's allusion to Cocteau's *Le Sang d'un Poète/The Blood of a Poet* (1930).

Another surrealistic scene occurs in *Evil Dead II* when Ash tries to sit in a chair after "hunting" his severed hand using a shotgun. The chair collapses and a fun-house atmosphere ensues in which the deer head, a lamp, books, cabinets, lampshades—every object in the room—

laughs at him. Ash joins in the laughter, although his sounds quickly turn to howls of horror.

In all three films, as is befitting such a relentless narrative of demons pursuing humans as the latter fight for their lives and souls, the camera work itself is charged with expressionistic verve. After an exhilarating attack in *Evil Dead II,* with Ash being hurtled backward through the forest and briefly possessed by the evil force, a slow montage follows as he lies unconscious in a puddle, showing him in various positions over a length of time. A moment of calm occurs as he comes to and looks around at the still and silent woods. The camera pans across cabin, car, woods, and back to Ash, shifting perspective from Ash's point of view to a view *of* him, and thus simultaneously creates a sense of connection and of disjunction. Only when "Join us!" sounds from the woods does the film bolt into action again as Ash tries, of course unsuccessfully, to leave in the car.

Foreshadowing is another means by which Raimi enriches his trilogy. Many horror films dispense with it, working merely on the principle of one unexpected shock after another. Others are heavy-handed in symbolic or verbal foreshadowing, a classic example of the latter being Johnny teasing his sister in the cemetery as what would turn out to be a zombie approaches them in *Night of the Living Dead,* "He's coming to get you, Barbara! He's dead! And he's going to get you." There is surprising depth and subtlety to the foreshadowing that Raimi works into the *Evil Dead* trilogy. If viewers look carefully, they will see everything prepared for and hinted at. For instance, in the first film Scotty's initial glance around the cabin upon entering lingers a moment each upon the deer head, mirror, and clock that later figure prominently; the shovel that Ash will use to bury his friends' corpses leans against the wall in the background as Scotty inspects the woodshed. When Ash tries to leave by car and faces a destroyed bridge in the second film, its five iron girders twisted up like fingers, he says, "I've got to get a grip on myself," anticipating how his own possessed hand will indeed grab onto his head. An important foreshadowing that becomes a motif throughout all the films is the square-shaped book-face, alluding to the *Necronomicon.* In *The Evil Dead,* Cheryl finds her hand possessed as she is sketching; it scrawls out a blockish and sinister face. Raimi cuts from this shot to the cabin's rattling basement trap door, upon which a chain lies in a square formation. In *Evil Dead II,* the chain Ash uses to fish for and fling the *Necronomicon* into the fireplace had been lying on the floor in the shape of the book-face; earlier Linda's crystal pendant necklace had been lying in the same configuration on the hearthrug. The face appears yet again at the end of that film when the cabin door is shown bearing two holes the demonized Cheryl earlier had punched through it from the outside to grab Ash within; now the evil force knocks down the door-face and rushes toward Ash.

A wide array of such recurring motifs connect the films and develop their plots, most overtly in the second and third films. The treatment can be simple, as in *Army of Darkness* when a man is thrown into a pit as sacrifice to the force of the evil dead and a fountain of blood comes up, echoing the moment in *Evil Dead II* when Henrietta Knowby's demonized corpse had pulled Jake into the basement and a geyser of blood shot out. At other times it is more integral to the plot, as in *Evil Dead II* when a box holding the *Necronomicon* crashes and breaks to show viewers those pages of the book that refer to "The Hero from the Sky," a foreshadowing of the end of this film and of the start of *Army of Darkness,* when Ash drops out of the sky into the mythomedieval world. Annie Knowby translates from the book to explain that whereas reciting the first passage in the book invokes the evil dead, "recitation of the second passage creates a kind of rift of time and space; and the physical manifestation of this dark spirit can be forced back into the rift." This idea of forcing the dark spirit back in time connects the second and third films and also helps to codify the freewheeling irrationalism of the first *Evil Dead* by giving the source of horror a basis in some sort of system. The voice-over at the beginning of *Evil Dead II* notes that the *Necronomicon* disappeared in A.D. 1300; *Army of Darkness* opens with Ash stating that he is in the year A.D. 1300. Thus Raimi lets an actual plot, or the semblance of one, take tentative shape—a plot that still allows for bizarre shifts of action and reaction, and even encourages them. At the end of *Evil Dead II,* while the face of a huge demon fills the doorway, Annie Knowby manages to finish reading the passages to dispel the evil dead, even though Ash's severed hand has stabbed her in the back. An abyss appears, sucking in Ash's car and the *Necronomicon,* and finally Ash himself, taking him into that mythomedieval past complete with knights and a flying dragonlike demon, which he kills with his shotgun. "Hail he who came from the sky!" the knights cry. *Army of Darkness* in turn opens with Ash landing in a mythomedieval land where knights surround him—but this time there is no flying demon to slay. Raimi's narrative disjunctions from film to film provide a conditional revision of what came before, further dislocating ordinary reality in a playful, ad hoc manner. So instead of hero, Ash becomes prisoner.

Raimi uses physical objects to connect the films, sometimes in a straightforward manner, as with the tape recorder or the crystal necklace and Michigan State clothing Ash's girlfriend wears in the first two films. At other times he makes an object the vehicle for delivering his special blend of horror, humor, and poetry. A mirror figures in all three films, providing a surreal moment in the first, as noted earlier, when Ash puts his hand into it, and offering comic relief in the second when Ash's mirror image leans out, grabs him by the collar, and says, "I'm fine? I don't think so. We just cut up our girlfriend with a chainsaw. Does that sound fine?" The image retreats and Ash gives a quick double-take at the mirror. In the third film a windmill replaces the cabin as a structure where peculiar things happen, and the mirror plays its most active part. Ash sees a reflection of his former self, in his own time period, and rushes the mirror in an Alice-like attempt to go through the looking glass and back to his own world. Instead, the mirror breaks, whereupon reflections of him come to life from the shards and become little Ashes who attack him viciously, with much laughter—a nice twist on the horror convention of a creature being blown to bits and dividing into numerous monsters to be fought, such as in *Blood Beach* (1981). Slipping on the pieces of glass, Ash wakes to find that his little selves have tied him down like Gulliver, affording Raimi the opportunity to push the concept to its absurd limits.

One homunculus dives into his mouth and moves into different parts of his body, so a deranged Ash asks, "How about some hot chocolate, huh?" and pours boiling water down his throat to kill it. But the invader grows, first erupting as a second head, with the result that Ash fights himself in classic Three Stooges fashion. Then it splits from Ash to become a complete and separate body, an evil twin who dances a jig and taunts, "I'm Bad Ash, and you're Good Ash. You're Little Goody Two-Shoes." Ash shoots the other in the face, saying flatly, "Good. Bad. I'm the guy with the gun." Such an attitude on the part of the protagonist might cause some viewers to extract a message Raimi most likely did not intend: Forced repeatedly into acts of murder and dismemberment of friends, as well as into mutilating his own body, by the third film in the series Ash's sense of a moral code has been severely challenged.

Although the *Evil Dead* movies have provoked a fair bit of civic-minded outrage, it is difficult to imagine them being any kind of threat to society. What other horror films gain so much of their power by poking fun at themselves and their genre? From the first explicitly violent act in *The Evil Dead,* when Ash's demonized sister gouges his girlfriend's ankle with a pencil, to the gruesome yet comic transference in *Evil Dead II,* when one of Henrietta Knowby's eyeballs flies out of its socket and into Bobbie Joe's mouth, to Bad Ash being catapulted from a castle in *Army of Darkness,* Raimi revels as much in mischief as in mayhem. In the first film, a possessed Linda taunts Ash by sitting in a doorway going "Hee, hee, hee," which so provokes Ash's ire that he smacks her several times—*hard*—to shut her up. Later, after she rises from the grave he has put her in, Ash hits her with a heavy beam and, laughing, she raises him up on it and tosses him onto her grave. Gore and humor blend when Ash decapitates her and her body spurts blood on him as she simultaneously strangles him and squirms lasciviously on top of him. In *Evil Dead II* Linda laughs that evil dead laughter until Ash whacks off her head with a shovel. Misogynistic? Promoting physical abuse? Advocating murder and dismemberment? Hardly. In the world of the evil dead, the end justifies the means. Raimi's central theme is that self-preservation—survival at any cost—is the most fundamental ethos. Self-sacrifice is for ninnies.

That this is not your average horror film violence is further evidenced by a scene in *Army of Darkness* when Ash's face becomes stuck to a stove while his little selves brutally attack him; he uses a small coal shovel to scrape his face off the hot metal. Another classic moment is when Linda's headless body tries to attack Ash with a chainsaw in *Evil Dead II.* He knocks the saw back *into* her neck, resulting in a lot of splattering blood as Linda cuts herself in half. But perhaps the greatest moment occurs in the same film when Ash's infected hand goes berserk, taking on a life of its own and gripping his face. "You bastards, you dirty bastards," he says, amid great physical comedy: the hand smacks Ash's head on the kitchen counter, throws him to the floor, smashes crockery on his head, and punches him in the gut and face. All the while munchkinlike voices twitter with mocking laughter. The camera focuses on a butcher knife. Gleefully proclaiming "Knife!" the hand crawls toward it, dragging Ash's unconscious body along over the broken pottery. Ash interrupts his hand's progress by pinning it to the floor with another kitchen knife, saying, "That's right, who's laughing now?" Raimi then surpasses himself by having Ash pick up the chainsaw and *cut off* his own hand, repeating the line, "Who's laughing now?" as his face becomes drenched with his own blood. The hand lies there on the floor a few moments before Ash clamps a bucket over it, says, "Here's your new home," and strategically places a copy of *A Farewell to Arms* on the top of the pile of books he assembles to hold the bucket down.

These are Raimi's finest moments. In *Evil Dead II,* a beleaguered and solitary Ash hopes for sanctuary in the cabin, but instead the piano plays itself, causing him to cry over sweet memories of Linda. This sentimental moment gets thoroughly desecrated when a barrier Ash had built over the window collapses. He sees his girlfriend's headless corpse rise out of the grave to pirouette, execute a kind of *grande révérence* to receive her head and rejoin it to her body, then give new meaning to the dance technique of "spotting" by making her body spin around while her head remains stationary, looking straight ahead at Ash. She finishes her routine by taking a tree as her dance partner, straddling a branch erotically. Raimi uses such stop-motion animation frequently, perhaps most amusingly in *Army of Darkness* to depict a battalion of the dead rising, where it is like *Sinbad and the Eye of the Tiger* (1977) effects specialist Ray Harryhausen on bad acid. The raised-dead skeletons are a wonderful combination of poetic effects and amusing gags, with the undead saying things such as, "That's right, sir!" and "My God, let's give them what for!" to their leader in a parody of military bluster. They march along to fife and drum, which Raimi has substituted with a leg-bone fife and a drum set made out of femurs and skulls.

Throughout, the ironic and even demented dialogue helps to balance the films' visual exuberance. Shortly after Linda's corpse's ballet, her severed head drops into Ash's lap as he sits in a chair, saying, "Hello lover," before biting onto his hand. He tries to beat her head off of his hand with a book, then by smacking it against the wall, until, in a moment of inspiration, he says, "Woodshed!" En route he smacks the head against a tree for good measure and, once in the shed, puts the head in a vise, where it says, "Even now we have your darling Linda's soul. She suffers in torment," evoking Ash's hilarious response, "You're going down!" As he staggers back to the cabin after sawing her head in half, he looks at his bloodied clothing and laments, "Oh geez."

In *Army of Darkness* Ash's now anachronistic way of talking provides much campy dialogue and action. He taunts a captor, "You know your shoelace is untied," and despite the fact that the warrior's boots have no shoelaces, he looks down, providing Ash with the opportunity to punch him. Assuming a position of power thanks to his advanced weapons, he addresses the crowd: "All right you primitive screwheads, listen up. See this? This is my *boom-stick!* It's a twelve-gauge double-barreled Remington, S-Mart's top of the line. You'll find this in the sporting goods department." This is total sales prattle, but with a sinister edge, close to a psychotic breakdown. When seducing a woman, Ash says, "Give me some sugar, baby!" In the same film, he finally reaches the cemetery where the *Necronomicon* lies, only to find *three* identical books on the stone altar. He opens one and gets sucked into a vacuum, climbing back out with his face contorted cartoonishly to proclaim, "Whoa! Wrong book." As he reaches for the second one, the mouth on its cover bites his hand and the book flies about, attacking him like a bat. "Oh, you! I'll get back to you!" Ash tosses out toward it, looking at the third book and saying, "Seems fairly obvious." Before opening it, he remembers to recite the incantation, "Klaatu Barata Niktu," Raimi's overt reference to *The Day the Earth Stood Still* (1951). But because he had not repeated the phrase three times as the Wiseman had requested when he was teaching it to him (an allusion to the scene in which the Michael Rennie character makes Patricia Neal repeat it), Ash cannot remember the last word and tries "Necktie, Necturn, Nickle," reflecting, "It's an N word. It was definitely an N word." He looks around like a naughty schoolboy who failed to prepare his lessons, then botches the incantation, coughing to cover up what should be "Niktu"—and of course all hell breaks loose: A storm arises over the entire country, skeletons' arms reach out of their graves, and Bad Ash arises to lead an army of the dead. Near the end of the movie Wiseman reminds Ash that he must recite the words *exactly* to wake up in his own time, and when Ash does make it back, a fellow S-Mart employee (played by Ted Raimi) asks, "Did you say the words right this time?" He testily replies, "Maybe I didn't say every tiny little syllable, no, but basically I said them, yeah." Next viewers see him fighting a customer who has turned into a demon and is screaming, "I'll swallow your soul!"

Given the trilogy as a whole, the other employee's words "this time" imply that Ash repeatedly goes through nightmarish trips to the mythomedieval land, which would be just his luck.

This implication of eternal recurrence is more than a joke at Ash's expense, for Ash is a parody of the archetypal hero, as outlined in Joseph Campbell's *The Hero with a Thousand Faces;* he is Seigfried without the ring, Tristan without a cause. For all his fortitude, his resourcefulness, and his square-jawed good looks, he represents the man who has atrocity rather than greatness thrust upon him. Ash can keep only half a step ahead of the violence crashing in all around him. He survives, and even grows stronger, if not smarter. But he is horribly, and hilariously, broken. The key comic element in all three films arises out of his hysterical, panicked attempts to struggle against the unconquerable invading force of the evil dead.

Certainly the *Evil Dead* films can be seen as childish in their approach to characterization, plot structure, and questions of taste, but intrinsic to that childishness is the grand playfulness of their assault on the senses. The crude violence of these movies is essential to their brilliance, in a similar way to George A. Romero's *Living Dead* films, or even so established an American classic as David Lynch's *Blue Velvet.* Inseparable from the vitality of the *Evil Dead* trilogy is the tastelessness, the gratuitous nastiness, and the gallows humor, all of which pervade virtually every scene, and all of which seem as validly satirical of the vanity of human wishes as, say, the work of the nineteenth-century American writers Ambrose Bierce and Edgar Allan Poe, or the comedy of Monty Python.

One can empathize with Raimi's desire to move on and make "grown-up" narratives, yet nonetheless lament the eclipsing of the inventive and poetic imagination at work in the *Evil Dead* trilogy. Following the trilogy and the almost equally wild *Darkman* (1990), in which a disfigured scientist dons synthetic skin to gain revenge against the villains who blew up him and his laboratory, Raimi directed *A Simple Plan* (1998), a realistic thriller marked by solid characterization and nuanced acting. Although Raimi had wanted to direct the movie from the start, he was not Scott Rudin's choice and got onto the project only after John Boorman left it (Mead, 1998). When discussing his objective in filming *A Simple Plan,* Raimi remarked that although he values the artfulness of the horror genre, as a viewer he prefers stories about real people (Mead, 1998). Despite this, as

Rebecca Mead observes about *A Simple Plan*'s cockpit scene, "For all Raimi's talk about the power of character, he knows exactly what to do with a pilot's decomposing corpse, a trapped, thrashing black crow, a lot of dark, cold metal, and a camera to leave his audience aghast with anxiety" (1998: 43).

The mainstream movie industry then embraced him fully in its clammy dead hands with a Kevin Costner baseball vehicle titled *For Love of the Game* (1999). That Raimi wants to expand his art and develop a subtler approach to it is commendable. Unfortunately, the image of a mildly troubled baseball player batting away toward victory can never compare with that of Ash laughing maniacally as he saws off his own hand to save himself.

Swinging from that pastoral mishap back to genres where he clearly shows more skill and authority, Raimi has directed *The Gift* (2000), a horror film, and *Spider-Man* (2002), featuring the classic Marvel Comics superhero. *The Gift* opens with a pan across the water of a foggy swampland, reminiscent of the eerie shots of the woods in the first two *Evil Dead* movies. The film concerns a psychic whose powers solve a murder case, and her visions, especially of the water-logged corpse, are delivered in startling, lightning-quick flashes that demonstrate Raimi's agility at infusing the camerawork required for a suspense thriller with touches of horror film techniques. As Tim Burton's *Batman* (1989) had featured the Caped Crusader's most charismatic arch-foe, the Joker, so Raimi's *Spider-Man* zeroed in on the Green Goblin. Willem Dafoe portrays the madman as a hyperactive split personality, with energy and ambition to burn for at least two lives. He thrives as both an endlessly calculating businessman and a maniacal supervillain; in short, two monsters in one, divided. The "responsible father" communicates with his alter ego through a mirror, echoing Ash's confrontation with his evil twin in *Evil Dead II*.

Camerawork and certain motifs earmark a Sam Raimi product, the legacy of his earlier immersion in horror filmmaking. His initial attempt to cash in on making genre films led to an acquired sensibility for their artistic possibilities. If the *Evil Dead* trilogy were nothing more than a training ground for a director who would go on to prove himself adept at making a variety of movies, their study would be worthwhile. That they in themselves are such rich exemplars of their genre makes their analysis imperative for any serious student of filmmaking, and makes one long for a return to childishness.

Chapter 4

The Darkness Is Not the Devil: Atheism and "The Death of Affect" in the Films of David Cronenberg

Though an atheist, in his mature work David Cronenberg continually presents a convergence or fusion of science and technology with quasi-religious themes, motifs, and structures. This can take the form of the birth of the "New Flesh" in *Videodrome* (1983), "purifying" in *The Fly* (1986), or a joining of machine and body in *Crash* (1996). His work does not exhibit the modernist conception of spiritual values gained through art, but instead an inner exploration of the self through ritualistic science or pseudoscience. There can be ritual without religion, and Cronenberg's references to religion do seem to deal more with ritual than with spirituality. However, at the same time there is a clear rejection of any theism, there is an attempt to create some kind of spiritual, or metaphysical, discipline. There is a drive beyond ritual, which results in a spiritual upheaval. There is such a longing in his characters; they need to relate on a basic human level even as they try to elevate beyond. In this way, atheism and what J. G. Ballard has called "the death of affect" are combined with a redemptive quality.

In the introduction to the French edition of his 1973 novel *Crash,* J. G. Ballard wrote, "Voyeurism, self-disgust, the infantile basis of our dreams and longings—these diseases of the psyche have now culminated in the most terrifying casualty of the century: the death of affect" (1985: 1). He goes on to explain,

> This demise of feeling and emotion has paved the way for all our most real and tender pleasures—in the excitements of pain and mutilation; in sex as the perfect arena, like a culture bed of sterile

pus, for all the veronicas of our own perversions; in our moral freedom to pursue our own psychopathology as a game. (1985: 1)

Ruminating on how the role of the writer has changed, Ballard declares, "He has no moral stance. . . . His role is that of the scientist, whether on safari or in his laboratory, faced with a completely unknown terrain or subject" (1985: 5-6).

Although Cronenberg might not agree with all of this, the same general fascination with a civilization's decline as a possible opening to further human development recurs constantly in the filmmaker's work, emerging and erupting in a sort of metastasis. The metaphor is apt, since his early films considered disease as a step in evolution, a sort of venereal evolution. Cronenberg's initial studies in college had been in the sciences, and his biographer Peter Morris notes that emergent evolutionism—the theory that "biological novelties emerged" through leaps in the evolutionary process—is an important influence in the themes of his films (Morris, 1994: 24). As Cronenberg explains it,

> It's about trying to understand interrelationships among organisms, even those we perceive as disease. To understand it from the disease's point of view, it's just a matter of life. . . . For them, it's very positive when they take over your body and destroy you. It's a triumph. It's all part of trying to reverse the normal understanding of what goes on physically, psychologically and biologically to us. (cited in Rodley, 1992: 82)

The sociosexual parasites of *Shivers* (1975) and the mutation of flesh in *Rabid* (1977) lurk behind his later films, as the body evolves through a fusion with technology: the cassettes inserted into Renn's body in *Videodrome,* the merging of the telepod and Brundlefly in *The Fly,* the idea that the body needs to change to fit the gynecological implements in *Dead Ringers* (1988). By the time he made *Crash,* Cronenberg seemed primed for the merging to be successful. There the characters hope for fusion and make obsessive attempts for it, fetishizing the pain and trauma of automobile collision as they join both with machine and other humans. With *eXistenZ* (1999), Cronenberg updated the videocassette technology from *Videodrome* and depicted it as being widely available: People have bioports installed at the bases of their spines so that they can plug into a game pod and enter a virtual reality. By the end of the movie, the very concept of reality is virtual.

Cronenberg says he does not feel connection with most other directors; he saw a lot of films but was not a student of them in the way of, say, Martin Scorsese. As he put it in an interview, "I suppose I was just consuming them, rather than studying them" (cited in Rodley, 1992: 153). He claims a more literary background, having enjoyed English as much as science in high school and switching his major from science to English language and literature in college (Morris, 1994). Given his interests, it is not surprising to find Cronenberg making use of the recurring figure of the mad scientist or doctor, simultaneously a reference to and departure from the nineteenth-century literary stock character. He has said, "I think the best scientists are as mad, creative and eccentric as writers and artists of any kind. I feel a lot of empathy for doctors and scientists. I often feel that they are my persona in my films" (cited in Rodley, 1992: 5). In *Frankenstein,* Mary Shelley gave readers a scientist trying to create human life; and although the theme of scientist-as-god is a bit hackneyed, Cronenberg pursues it in intriguing ways, stating,

> You have to believe in God before you can say there are things that man was not meant to know. I don't think there's anything man wasn't meant to know. There are just some stupid things that people shouldn't do. In another way, everybody's a mad scientist, and life is their lab. (cited in Rodley, 1992: 7)

This statement shows how positively the filmmaker views the mutations and apparent self-destructions that pervade his movies. Cronenberg's scientists are messianic figures leading the way into the next stage, one that hopes to free the body of its current limitations, and by doing so free the mind as well.

The Brood (1979) demonstrates a maturation of Cronenberg's work, a move from exploitation films—albeit horrifying ones—such as *Rabid* and *Shivers.* It opens with a demonstration of an experimental technique, as *Scanners* (1981) and *eXistenZ* would later. Dr. Hal Raglan (Oliver Reed), founder of the Somafree Institute of Psychoplasmics, has gathered an audience of potential clients to witness a therapy session. His technique is to encourage—push, really—his patients to pursue their dark emotions, emotions rooted in childhood yet still quite active, however repressed, in the adult. Telling them to "go all the way through it to the end," Raglan perseveres until his patients' anguish and anger manifests itself physically, via a rash, cancer, or, in the case of his most successful patient, Nola Carveth (Samantha Eggar), the "birth" of child-sized beings—the Brood—who act out her emotions by killing people Nola has strong negative feelings toward. The word *nola* is Low or Late Latin for "a little bell," and Nola does indeed ring as a warning that Dr. Raglan is pursuing something that turns out to be lethal, to himself as well as others.

The Shape of Rage is the title of Raglan's book on psychoplasmics, and it aptly describes his philosophy. Frank Carveth (Art Hindle), whose name indicates his desire to cut through any nonsense and get to the truth, calls Raglan an emotional opportunist, someone who preys on his patients' weaknesses; in this case, Frank's wife, as the couple undergoes a divorce. The pawn in the separation is their daughter Candice, often called Candy. Truth, sweet, trite—the various connotations of her name further push Cronenberg's themes. At one point Nola worries that she is trying to turn Candy into a "Baby Nola," which, given Nola's past, is frightening indeed. As a child, Nola was physically and verbally abused by her mother, who beat her, scratched her, and threw her down the stairs. The mother, Julianna, is an alcoholic in complete denial. She responds to Candy's query, prompted by a photograph, about why her mother was hospitalized so frequently as a child: "Some days she would wake up and she'd be covered with big ugly bumps." Since Nola is in session with Dr. Raglan when this conversation takes place, at this point the Brood enter Julianna's home and bludgeon her to death with a meat mallet. Cronenberg inserts a visual joke into the scene where the Brood are ransacking the kitchen prior to the murder: They knock a box of Shreddies cereal out of a cabinet. That joke and the cute little snowsuits the Brood wear evoke emotions in the viewer that are directly opposed to those evoked while watching the brutal killings.

The second victim of Nola's emotions is her father, as alcoholic as his former wife and as much in denial. Nola blames him for not protecting her, for looking away when she was beaten and pretending it was not happening; the Brood extract her revenge for this lapse of filial duty. The victim who might be said to suffer the most in this film, however, is the five-year-old Candy. Witnessing her grandmother's murder, her face is completely impassive; no emotion registers. After, she simply goes upstairs and falls asleep. The authorities warn Frank that such a deep sleep indicates Candy is repressing the bad experience and that he must "urge her to remember" the murder in order to deal with it. Soon, we see Frank photographing Candy's "wounds"—he thinks Nola is abusing her during the daughter's visitations to the institute, but the question arises of whether a Baby Nola is indeed emerging, whether seemingly dormant feelings are erupting physically. The scene is peculiarly disturbing in that Candy, looking out of a window with her back to her father, is naked from the waist up. Her turned-down dress and the large artificial flower she holds suggest a pornographic photo shoot, alluding at the least to various kinds of potential parental abuse and contributing to an underlying suggestion specifically of incestual abuse. In scenes when Frank is taking leave of his daughter, he kisses her directly on the mouth. Complicating this theme is Dr. Raglan's role-playing as parent to his patients, in Nola's case as both her "daddy" and the father of her Brood; that he kisses her on the mouth in a session as her "daddy" creates the effect of a moral hall of mirrors.

Indeed, Dr. Raglan's patients' jealousy of one another, their vying for his attention, and their "addiction" to his treatment, as one of them describes it, underscores Cronenberg's overarching theme of coveting, perhaps most obviously seen in Nola and Frank's struggle to be sole parent to Candy. (Cronenberg has stated that he wrote *The Brood* during his custody battle for his daughter. His wife had joined a cult in California [Rodley, 1992].) "Nola's the queen bee!" former patient Mike laments while telling Frank how Raglan has dismissed all his patients but Nola. Nola's jealousy extends to Candy's school teacher, whom Frank invited over to dinner one evening and told, reflecting on what he tells himself about his relationship with Nola, "You got involved with a woman who married you for your sanity, hoping it would rub off. Instead it started to work the other way." The Brood enters Candy's classroom, carefully guiding that child out of the room before murdering the teacher, one of the more unusual depictions of maternal protection in cinema. When the final murder by the Brood occurs, that of Dr. Raglan, Candy watches with her hands over her ears, actively trying to block out what she hears. The Brood is destroyed when Frank kills Nola to save Candy. As father and daughter drive away from the institute, lesions begin to appear on Candy's forearm.

Everything is doomed in this film. The grandparents' marriage, Frank and Nola's marriage, a relationship between Frank and Candy's teacher. Candy is lost from the start, her catatonic state indicating that she cannot be reached and hence cannot be saved. Given that Frank tells Candy at the end, "We're going home," and she asks, "So where is that?" the father might be lost as well. *The Brood* is about unavoidable losses and the futile attempts to evade them. It stands in sharp contrast to other Cronenberg films portraying annihilatory situations that lead to redemption, such as *Videodrome* and *Naked Lunch* (1991).

Videodrome gives viewers Max Renn (James Woods), owner of Civic TV, who thinks Asian porn videos are "too soft" and is looking for something that will "break through," something "tough" to air on Channel 83. As he speaks, viewers see a poster behind him with the image of a big hand and the caption, "Something waits in the darkness." Indeed it does, for Renn finds a show apparently broadcast from Pittsburgh, "Videodrome," a torture, murder, and mutilation vehicle, and exclaims, "You can't take your eyes off it!" Renn believes in broadcasting shows that range from soft-core porn to hard-core violence because he sees them as positive outlets for viewers' frustrations and fantasies. During a three-way interview on a talk show involving Renn and Professor Brian O'Blivion (whom we later find out was one of the creators of "Videodrome"), when the host says "desensitization" in the context of her belief that sexual and violent television shows lead to dehumanization, O'Blivion's televised image glances sharply at her. This becomes eerie in retrospect when viewers find out that O'Blivion was dead by that point and his image and words are prerecorded, not broadcast live.

As he slowly learns more about it, Renn swings between wanting to expose and wanting to be part of "Videodrome," unlike his girlfriend, Nicki (Deborah Harry), who is immediately into it, is *there.* "Can't you get it any clearer?" she asks when they are watching the show. "I like it. It turns me on. . . . I wonder how you get to be a contestant on this show." Although he enjoys viewing it, Renn is taken aback at her wanting to participate in the show, surprised too to find out that she is willing to be cut with a knife. The first time the couple had sex the scene became like the "Videodrome" set, with a tactile, claylike wall in the background. This makes sense to viewers later when they learn that, like O'Blivion, Nicki too is already dead and

Renn has begun the hallucinations that the "Videodrome" signal induces.

When he finds out it is real "snuff" TV, Renn comes to understand that, as his friend Masha warns, "'Videodrome' is definitely not meant for public consumption." The remark underscores the isolationist motif in Cronenberg's work. Woods's performance is nuanced and subtle in a way one does not commonly associate with James Woods, which accords with his being a viewer of rather than contestant on "Videodrome," as well as his being an agent of "Videodrome," performing its will, as is slowly revealed over the course of the movie. For "Videodrome" is more than a television show; it is a conspiracy. Masha observes, "It has something you don't, Max. It has a philosophy, and that is what makes it dangerous." The philosophy was that of Brian O'Blivion, and Renn is soon drawn to O'Blivion's Cathode Ray Mission, where derelict supplicants watch television incessantly in their private cubicles, getting their dose of what "helps patch the homeless back into the world's mixing board," as O'Blivion's daughter remarks paradoxically. Renn discovers what is left of O'Blivion: a huge library of videotapes, of which O'Blivion often made several a day. Bianca O'Blivion (Sonja Smits), whose first name suggests the white noise of a channel when it is not broadcasting, explains about her father, "The monologue is his preferred form of discourse."

Renn descends into a kind of psychosis, thinking he has hit his work assistant when she comes to his apartment to deliver one of O'Blivion's videocassettes, seeing Nicki at the time of the imaginary blow, and, after the assistant leaves, believing for a moment that the videocassette pulsates. Renn watches the tape and hears more of O'Blivion's philosophy:

> The battle for the mind of North America will be fought in the video arena, the videodrome. The television screen is the retina of the mind's eye. Therefore, the television screen is part of the physical structure of the brain. Therefore, whatever appears on the television screen emerges as raw experience for those who watch it. Therefore, television is reality and reality is less than television.

"Your reality is already half illusion," O'Blivion tells Renn. He also reveals that he believes that television images caused his brain tumor, cryptically saying that when the tumor was removed it was called

Videodrome. "I was 'Videodrome''s first victim," he states proudly. It is fairly clear to viewers that Renn is becoming another victim of "Videodrome," for at this point the television set pulsates erotically, breathes, and sighs while Nicki's image croons, "I want you, Max. Come to me," as prelude to Renn's caressing the set and entering Nicki's giant lips through the now-bulbous screen.

Renn tells Bianca that watching "Videodrome" seems to have set off a series of hallucinations, only to learn that the videodrome signal has induced a brain tumor in him that is creating them. Professor O'Blivion had seen "Videodrome" as "the next phase in the evolution of man as a technological animal," Bianca explains. "At the end he was convinced that public life on television was more real than private life in the flesh. He wasn't afraid to let his body die," a remark that foreshadows Renn's own redemptive death. To learn about his "'Videodrome' problem," Renn watches more of O'Blivion's tapes —with a pistol in hand that he uses to scratch his stomach. O'Blivion says,

> I think that massive doses of "Videodrome" signal will ulti-
> mately create a new growth of the human brain, which will pro-
> duce and control hallucination to the point that it will change
> human reality. After all, there is nothing real outside our percep-
> tion of reality, is there? You can see that, can't you?

Cronenberg then delivers a shocking image: An opening, a slot— really an orifice—appears in Renn's stomach, into which he puts his hand and the gun. When he pulls his hand out and the opening seals up, the gun is left inside.

Renn is contacted by Barry Convex, the aptly named owner of Spectacular Optical, a company that makes eyeglasses and lenses, but also "Videodrome." He wants to record Renn's hallucination for analysis because while all other test subjects of "Videodrome" have needed intensive psychiatric treatment, Renn is still highly functional. Clamping on headgear reminiscent of early virtual reality equipment, Convex explains that watching a "little S&M" should trigger hallucinations. "That's why our 'Videodrome' show is so strange," he notes. "Something to do with the effects of exposure to violence on the nervous system. It opens up receptors in the brain and the spine, and then allows the 'Videodrome' signal to sink in." And sink in it does, for Renn appears to be on the "Videodrome" set with

Nicki, who suddenly is inside a television that Renn whips with a cat-o'-nine-tails; the image turns into Masha in bondage, and Renn appears to wake up in his bed to the white noise of the television—only to hallucinate that Masha's bloody corpse is beside him.

Renn learns that his assistant, Harlan (Cronenberg's little tribute to Harlan Ellison), has been an agent of "Videodrome," which was never broadcast—rather than tapping into a signal, Harlan has been playing tapes for two years. Barry Convex inserts a videocassette into Renn's stomach slot to program him to kill his partners and give Channel 83 over to Convex so that he can broadcast "Videodrome." Another Cronenbergian fusion of human and machine occurs when Renn observes his gun joining with his hand, becoming an organic, veined weapon. He is programmed to kill Bianca too, but she reveals how Convex and O'Blivion's other former partners in "Videodrome" had killed Nicki and used her image to seduce him. "'Videodrome' is death," she explains, changing his cassette to free him from the control of "Videodrome." "You've become something quite different from what you were," she notes. "You've become the video word made flesh. . . . You know what you have to do. Use the weapons they've given you to kill 'Videodrome.'" The two then chant, "Death to 'Videodrome.' Long live the New Flesh."

Cronenberg shows a different destructive aspect of the human-machine combination when Harlan tries to insert a videocassette into Renn's stomach slot and Harlan's hand and arm are eaten away as if by acid. Renn proceeds to the Spectacular Optical convention—the slogan of which is "Love comes in at the eye"—to kill Convex. On the run from the police, Renn goes to the harbor and boards a condemned barge. Hallucinating that he sees his own television set, he watches Nicki tell him, "I've learned that death is not the end. I can help you." "I don't know where I am now," Renn replies, "I'm having trouble finding my way around." "That's because you've gone just about as far as you can, with the way things are," she explains. He has hurt "Videodrome," but not destroyed it. "To do that you have to go on to the next phase . . . Your body has changed a lot, but it's only the beginning," Nicki explains, urging him to "go all the way," to achieve "total transformation." "To become the New Flesh, you first have to kill the old. . . . Don't be afraid to let your body die. Come to Nicki; I'll show you how," she cajoles. Renn watches an image of himself on television before a small fire, putting his gun hand to his head, saying

"Long live the New Flesh!" and shooting himself. The television set explodes and viscera and chunks of bloody flesh fly out of it. Viewers then see the same suicide scene that was televised ostensibly occurring in "real" life. The movie screen goes black.

As Max Renn demonstrates, even though Cronenberg's characters often are isolated from even their own feelings, they try to push through. His use of a very insular cast serves to echo the insularity of the characters. Cronenberg's remake of the 1958 movie *The Fly* allows him to emphasize this at the same time it transforms a wonderfully bad old horror movie into the next step in his film depictions of the death of affect. When given Charles Pogue's script, he rewrote it (save for one line of dialogue) and revised the characters as well (Morris, 1994). Brundle (Jeff Goldblum) represents both the hopeless antihero and the visionary scientist who uses the antihero. Brundle's first name is Seth, the son given to Adam and Eve after Abel's death. As a replacement child, Seth was the beginning of a new race. The name might also refer to the Egyptian god Seth, who represented evil and chaos for murdering his brother Osiris and dismembering his body. The name of Seth's girlfriend, Veronica (Geena Davis), suggests the legend of the woman who wiped the sweat from Jesus' face with her veil while he was carrying the cross; the cloth retained his image and, when discovered in St. Peter's Basilica in the eighth century, was hailed as the *vera iconica* ("the true image") of Jesus. Ostensibly, the cloth had certain healing powers (Walker, 1983). Given the role Seth wishes Veronica to play in helping purify him late in his "illness," as well as the allusion to the Christian triumvirate, her name has significant resonance.

Seth Brundle is a messianic figure, despite his saying in the middle of a sermon directed at Veronica, "Not to wax messianic." His version of scientific religion involves purification through teleportation. As he explains to Veronica in a coffee shop, "Why, it's like coffee being put through a filter. It's somehow a purifying process." Later he notes, "It's like a drug, but a perfectly pure and benign drug." An incredible homily comes when Brundle tries to convince Veronica to go through the transporter. "We'll be the perfect couple—the dynamic duo," he says excitedly, an allusion to a scientifically made Adam and Eve, and a suggestion that science can be a religion. Tellingly, Veronica retorts, "Don't give me that born-again teleportation crap." Brundle is off on a streak, though, and launches on:

You're afraid to dive into the plasma pool, aren't you? You're afraid to be destroyed and be re-created, aren't you? [Here Cronenberg echoes *Videodrome* and the New Flesh.] I'll bet you think that you woke me up about the flesh, don't you? But you only know society's straight line about the flesh. You can't penetrate beyond society's sick, gray fear of the flesh. Drink deep or taste not the plasma spring! See what I'm saying, I'm not just talking about sex and penetration, I'm talking about penetration beyond the veil of the flesh. A deep penetrating dive into the plasma pool.

Brundle has clearly dived into the pool, for his flylike metabolism causes him to devour candy bars and pick up a woman in a bar to satiate his relentless sexual appetite. "Are you a body builder?" she asks, awed at how he had won at arm wrestling by breaking the other man's arm. He replies, "I take them apart and then I put them back together again." When he comes out of the teleporter naked, like an Adam reborn, Cronenberg's allusion is impossible to miss: "I'm become free, I've been released, and you can't stand it," he says to Veronica. And Brundle certainly is evolving: His teeth come out, his fingernails come off, and his fingers ooze secretory acids. Four weeks after discovering he fused with a fly at the molecular level, Brundle asks Veronica to come see him. By this point he is using canes when upright and, in true mad scientist form, comments with interest on how things change every day for him, fascinated with the permutations he is going through even as they destroy him. He crawls on the ceiling while musing,

> I seem to be stricken by a disease with a purpose, wouldn't you say? Maybe not such a bad disease after all . . . The disease has just revealed its purpose. . . . I know what the disease wants. . . . It wants to turn me into something else. That's not too terrible, is it? Most people would give anything to be turned into something else. . . . I'm becoming something that never existed before. I'm becoming Brundlefly."

Brundle had always retreated from the outside world into his scientific vision; charming yet remote, he dealt with people only when he needed them. Now his vision, substantially altered though still intact, has been internalized, or, more specifically, he has become its incarnation. But Veronica has stirred his deepest feelings, and his last sign of human vulnerability is his fear for her. "Insects don't have politics," he tells Veronica. "They're very brutal. No compassion. No compromise. We can't trust the insect. I'd like to become the first insect politician." Then he says, "I'm an insect who dreamt he was a man, and loved it. But now the dream is over, and the insect is awake," which is a sharp reference to Gregor Samsa in Franz Kafka's "The Metamorphosis." Gregor awakens one morning to discover he has transformed into an insect, and although his human emotions grow over the course of the story, to his family he becomes "a creature," one that needs to be locked in a room until he dies (Kafka, 1979: 48). In Brundlefly's case, the image of the door to his warehouse apartment symbolizes for viewers his cutting himself off from humanity, and his apartment becomes like a cave or tomb, from which he banishes Veronica, warning her, "I'll hurt you if you stay."

Veronica is pregnant and wants to abort their child, fearing it will be deformed or degenerate once born, while Brundle desperately wants to preserve the last vestige of his humanity, so he leaves his apartment to abduct her from the hospital. Veronica's former lover and current editor, Stathis, who had arranged her abortion and accompanied her to the hospital (to see a gynecologist played by Cronenberg himself), now follows them, bringing along a shotgun. Brundle has set up a third teleporter and wants Veronica to be teleported so that he can be saved through joining physically with her and their unborn child. The computer had told him that the element of fly in him could be reduced by splicing with another, pure human. "We'll be the ultimate family," he pleads. "A family of three joined together in one body. More human than I am alone." An unholy trinity would be unified—through purification, a new flesh, a new race would be created. However, Brundle degenerates further until the fly under the human flesh emerges, forces Veronica into a teleporter, and enters one itself. Stathis had been incapacitated when Brundle vomited digestive acid on one of his hands and a foot, but he is able to shoot and sever the connection to Veronica's telepod. The angered Brundlefly breaks the glass window of his telepod but is halted from emerging by the completion of the teleportation process. Brundlefly has fused with his telepod and, part man-fly, part machine, by gesture the creature asks Veronica to shoot him, which she does.

Cronenberg embellished the premise of the original short story to include the fusion of human/fly with machine, letting his contemplation of science and technology play itself out. His version can be seen as a science-fiction allegory framed by a tragic love story, or vice versa. As Victor Frankenstein kills part of himself in killing his monstrous creation, so Brundlefly, with Veronica's despairing help, kills the monster he created: himself.

Dead Ringers is equally moving, though more complex. Insularity reaches its apogee in this film, with one actor (Jeremy Irons) playing twin brothers who are two intertwined entities from the womb to the barricaded examination room. The Mantle brothers' name resonates with meaning. The mantle is a religious garment, and while their red surgical robes suggest the menstrual blood associated with their profession, gynecology, the robes are priestly as well. At one point Elliot explains a surgery that medical students are observing, and the scene in the background of Beverly and his assistants operating looks like a religious ceremony around an altar. Mantle also suggests a yoke, a burden, and the development of the brothers' intertwining existence that viewers come to understand over the course of the film certainly indicates this meaning of their name. As well, given their profession as gynecologists, in the architectural term there is the suggestion of labia, as the entranceway to the vagina.

Cronenberg deals extensively with medical implements in *Dead Ringers*. The image over which the opening credits are run features the Mantle brothers' creative instruments displayed against a scarlet background. As undergraduates they invent what becomes a standard of gynecological medicine, the Mantle retractor—which their instructor had said might be "fine for a cadaver, but not a living woman." When Beverly has sex with Claire Niveau (Geneviève Bujold), a patient the two brothers share as a sexual partner—at first unbeknownst to her—he ties her to the bedstead with surgical tubing held by operating clamps. They seek out an artist to make their instruments for working on "mutant women" because their conceptions have "always been too radical" for medical implement companies. Indeed, the doctors want to re-create the female body. "No, no, there's nothing the matter with the instrument. It's the body. The woman's body was all wrong," complains Beverly, the visionary brother, when one of his gynecological instruments is criticized.

Over the course of his career, Cronenberg has modified and refined his basically phenomenological philosophy. The interrelation of the physical and psychological has progressed from the early mutation fantasies, à la *Shivers,* to the complications of *Dead Ringers'* conception of both the human body and the human being, and on to the diabolic conflations of flesh and psyche in the later movies *Crash* and *eXistenZ.*

In *Dead Ringers,* Claire, an actress who comes to Beverly because she wishes to become pregnant and female fertility is the Mantle brothers' specialization, is intriguing to him as a patient because she has a tripartite uterus, each with its own cervix. Elliot is the first to have sex with her, although he pretends to be Beverly when he does so. Elliot tells Bev that Claire is an actress who plays games. "You never know who she really is," he remarks, a telling phrase given the deceptive game the brothers play on her. Later in the movie Elliot tells Claire, "You contribute a confusing element to the Mantle brothers' saga, possibly a destructive one." Indeed she does, in numerous ways. She begins Bev's drug addiction by getting him to take the diet pills she abuses for their euphoric side effect. She asks Beverly why he has a woman's name, at which he becomes very testy. He is the more sensitive of the brothers, the one who cries; the one who is extremely upset when Claire discovers what has been going on and rejects them both; and the one who bends his head to be comforted like a child by a woman doctor whom Elliot has brought home for them to share sexually. Elliot is the aggressor in this last scene, and when Beverly tries to leave he calls out after him, "Bev, stay with us. . . . Stay with *me,*" indicating that such an interaction—indeed, the whole fraternal relationship—involves a homoerotic connection. In the restaurant scene in which Claire discovers she has been having sex with both men, she flings at Elliot, "What's with you, chum? You can't get it up unless little brother's watching?" Elliot calls Bev "baby brother" throughout the movie, asserting his dominance and Bev's dependence on him.

Earlier, Claire had asked Beverly, upon learning he has a twin brother, "Are you identical psychologically?" "No, I wouldn't say that," is his reply, and this is apparent in the subtle physical differences Irons matches to their differences of personality. Yet at times the viewer can be confused. After this scene, Claire and Beverly have sex. Postcoital, Bev's hair falls into the style Elliot wears. Is this Elliot? In a gallery scene, Beverly remarks that the sculpture seems "cold and empty." The attendant responds, "You can call it empty, or you can call it clean. Sculpture, it's a question of the individual nervous system, I think." Beverly says, "Of course that presupposes one has an individual nervous system," a hint at the brothers' confusion of identities. At one point Claire asks Beverly if Elliot is jealous of her, if he is worried that she will steal Beverly away from him. She observes, "I think you two have never come to terms with the way it really does work between you." Beverly's reaction is to have a nightmare in which Claire, saying she'll separate the two brothers, eats through an umbilical-like link that joins them at the abdomen (hearkening back to the "birthing" imagery in *The Brood*).

When Beverly's drug problem lands him in the hospital and ruins his medical career, he expresses concern for how Elliot is getting on without him. "Don't worry about me. I'm not you," is Elliot's response. Nonetheless, Elliot becomes addicted to drugs when he takes stimulants to stay awake and watch over Bev after he is released from the hospital. A fellow doctor urges Elliot to remember he has a separate reputation and career, but Elliot declares that he and Bev are perceived as one person and will "go down the tubes" together, a cliché that resonates with meaning: fallopian tubes, surgical tubing, using surgical tubing to shoot up. Indeed, when the doctor continues, "You've got to cut yourself loose," Elliot tellingly observes, "Whatever is in his bloodstream goes directly into me." The brothers move willfully toward their end. "I just have to get synchronized," Elliot notes; "Once we're synchronized it will be easy." So the two work out a drug-taking schedule. Beverly has stolen their surgical tools from the artist's gallery, where they were on display, and declares that they are for separating Siamese twins. After reciting the story of the original Siamese twins in a sing-song voice that suggests he has done so many times, Beverly says, "I'm about to separate the Siamese twins," and eviscerates his brother, a celebratory evocation of his birthing nightmare. Awakening later to discover what he has done, he chants "Ellie, Ellie, Ellie" in a state of shock, then cleans himself up and leaves the clinic with a satchel. He telephones Claire but ultimately cannot be separated from Elliot, returning instead to the clinic to overdose so that the two brothers lie dead in a pietàlike formation.

Male, female, connection, individuality, identity, insularity of kin, involvement with others—Cronenberg deftly handles many issues and complexities in *Dead Ringers*. For all the clinical aspects of the script, it is a very humanistic film. Irons's performance as each of the twin brothers is brilliantly singular.

In an interview Cronenberg referred to *The Fly* as "metaphysical horror" (cited in Rodley, 1992: 134), along the lines of metaphysical poetry, "in which normally unharmonious elements are violently yoked together" (cited in Rodley, 1992: 131)—an allusion to Samuel Johnson's description of metaphysical poetry. This seems like a fairly apt term for his mature work, and for none more so than *Naked Lunch,* inspired by William S. Burroughs's 1959 book by the same title. Cronenberg had long been an avid reader of Burroughs and notes his influence several times in *Cronenberg on Cronenberg.* Chris Rodley sees the film *Naked Lunch* as "a fitting form of cinematic destiny," explaining, "Their nervous systems had been connected for years; both men shared the same nightmares and visions; both evinced a puritan disgust of the flesh (though at least one of them would deny this); both had been criticized and censored for their extreme imaginings" (1992: 157). Reflecting on his adaptation of the novel, Cronenberg says, "I didn't want it to be a movie about drugs, because I think Burroughs is more about addiction and manipulation and control. . . . By inventing my own drugs they would have internal, metaphorical connections attached to them, rather than external, social ones. . . . I also knew that I wanted it to be about writing: the act of writing and creating something that is dangerous to you" (cited in Rodley, 1992: 164-65).

The danger, even the treachery or self-betrayal, of writing as both a concept and a physical act brings focus to Cronenberg's screenplay. Summarizing the plot would be as foolhardy as actually attempting a movie version of the novel. Cronenberg's film uses Burroughs's life story as a sort of matrix through which to introduce themes and passages from *Naked Lunch* and other of Burroughs's writings. These volatile elements plunge the film headlong into a garish nightmare of paranoia and hallucination and, ultimately, the acceptance of these states as necessary and even beneficial. The obvious "mad scientist" figure here is Dr. Benway (Roy Scheider at his wryest), provider of the addictive centipede powder, except that the character is so peripheral. The main character, Bill Lee (Peter Weller), serves as the high scientist, coldly studying himself and all around him as he horribly, inexorably, becomes a writer. Therein lies perhaps the most disturbing subtext of the screenplay. In 1951, Burroughs accidentally killed his wife, Joan, by shooting her in the head during a drunken "William Tell" party game. Not long after that, he began to write in earnest. Cronenberg makes a connection between that homicide and the process of becoming a writer. The implied question is, could that accidental killing have been Burroughs's literary inspiration? The question is complicated by Burroughs's later insistence, quoted in the film, that "there are no accidents."

Of course, Cronenberg is not making a forensics case. He brings this material to bear on the nature of will and creativity. Writers are notoriously both willful and passive, egocentric and insecure. Frequently, they describe the need to write as a compulsion. Many writers, Burroughs included, have mentioned a sense of being dictated to. And yet writing *is* a willful action, a presumptive release of emotions and ideas. Bill Lee's ambivalent passivity is the catalyst for his transformation, a point on which his main writing machine, Clark-Nova, never tires of harping. Early on in their relationship it says, "I want you to type a few words into me. Words that I'll dictate to you." Later it trips Lee up by explaining, "I've been instructed to reveal to you that you were programmed to kill your wife. . . . It was not an act of free will on your part." This treacherous codependence between human and machine becomes the central metaphor or trope of *Naked Lunch*. Lee learns vital information (which turns out to be useless) from the writing machine he is supposed to be communicating through; he also projects his horrific visions onto the machine, so that he does not have to take responsibility for them. After killing his wife, he pawns his pistol in exchange for a typewriter: the two great scourges of the West and, incidentally, Burrough's two favorite tools (or toys). At one point Lee fittingly remarks, "I understood writing could be dangerous. I didn't realize the danger came from the machinery."

Naked Lunch is the most literarily canny of Cronenberg's films. Not only did it serve as a unique tribute to a singularly influential contemporary writer but it also raises allusions to earlier influences, including "The Metamorphosis" once again when Joan Lee (Judy Davis) says of the bug powder she shoots up, "It's a Kafka high. You feel like a bug." More obscurely, the film shows Joan killing cockroaches by breathing on them and, later, Lee killing a centipede in the same fashion. Poison imbues their bodies, as in "Rappaccini's Daughter," a short story by Nathaniel Hawthorne in which a scientist experiments on his daughter and her suitor, making both toxic. Beatrice is restricted to living in a walled garden described as an "Eden of poisonous flowers" (Hawthorne, 1982: 995), and before long Giovanni too will become unsafe to the outside world. Beatrice kills a butterfly and Giovanni kills a spider in its web, each by breathing upon the insect. And as in Hawthorne's work, to say nothing of Burroughs's, the apparent setting of the text—in the film *Naked Lunch,* whether New York or, more obviously, Interzone—represents a mental state. Interior and exterior become irrelevant distinctions.

In *Crash,* the concept of the "writing machine," by which one defines and expresses himself or herself, becomes even more internal while at the same time it terrorizes the highways and underpasses of contemporary society. In his introduction to *Crash,* Ballard explained that his aim in writing science fiction was to explore inner space, "that psychological domain (manifest, for example, in surrealist painting) where the inner world of the mind and the outer world of reality meet and fuse" (1985: 3). In *Crash* this becomes a study of the characters' fetishistic obsession with automobile wrecks. "Do we see, in the car crash, a sinister portent of a nightmare marriage between sex and technology?" Ballard asks. "Will modern technology provide us with hitherto undreamed-of means for tapping our own psychopathologies? Is this harnessing of our innate perversity conceivably of benefit to us?" (1985: 6). One readily sees why Cronenberg was drawn to make a film based on Ballard's novel, as well as to acting in it as an auto wreck salesman.

Although the film is remarkably faithful to the novel—if anything, it tones down the perverse and inflammatory qualities—Cronenberg shapes his own vision out of Ballard's words, creating a work that is both adaptation and interpretation. In short, a distillation. *Crash* seems far more realistic than *Naked Lunch* yet presents a more convincingly insular world of psychosis; an overstimulated, hypermediated world where pain is the common currency of interaction. It serves as a necessary stage of transformation and also as a means of emotional connection at the far curve of affect. The characters share a mutual alienation. From Ballard (James Spader) to Vaughan (Elias Koteas), they share a Romantic desire to connect with each other and with their enclosing environment in spite of their nearly completely dissociative conditions. Ballard and his wife, Catherine (Deborah Kara Unger), have been having extramarital affairs and sharing the details with each other. When Ballard, along with Dr. Helen Remington (Holly Hunter), is injured in a car crash that kills Remington's husband, his life regains some meaning—twisted meaning. He, Catherine, and Remington fall in with others, led by Vaughan, who are obsessed with the erotic potential of car crashes.

These people pursue their obsessions through a netherworld, a city-waste of inner space. They search for a meaningful iconography in a world of meaningless (or senseless) collision and impact, and find the fetishism of that violence the only viable connection, obsession the only reasonable eschatology. Car and person form a symbiotic relation centered on predation. Not only is there the fusion of flesh and chrome, the startling geometries between human and machine, but, characteristic of Cronenberg's characters and scenarios while also staying true to Ballard's text, this fascination has imaginative outgrowths.

For instance, most of the characters view celebrity deaths as a means of potent transubstantiation. Vaughan's form of performance art is the reenactment of these deaths. He philosophizes that "the car crash is a fertilizing rather than a destructive event, a liberation of sexual energy that mediates the sexuality of those who have died with an intensity impossible in any other form." Vaughan drives a black vintage Lincoln Continental convertible, the same model Kennedy rode in when he was assassinated. This makes brilliant sense, given both Kennedy's priapic nature and his iconic status as a great American martyr. (It is worth noting that Ballard wrote a pastiche of Alfred Jarry's "The Crucifixion Considered as an Uphill Bicycle Race" titled "The Assassination of John Fitzgerald Kennedy Considered as a Downhill Motor Race.")

Vaughan manufactures the characters' drives and desires into a philosophy; he gives the madness a structure, calling it "a benevolent psychopathology." He is a new variation on the recurring mad scientist figure in Cronenberg's work, both one of the most playful and one of the most megalomaniacal. That tension comes through most clearly in a scene in which he has a tattoo depicting a wound made on his abdomen. He complains that the tattoo artist is making the tattoo "too clean," and in response to her assertion that medical tattoos are supposed to be clean, he explains, "This isn't a medical tattoo. This is a prophetic tattoo. Prophecy is dirty and ragged. Make it dirty and ragged." When the artist asks, "Prophetic? Is this personal prophecy or

global prophecy?" Vaughan responds, "There's no difference." Con-
man lunatics are the poor cousins of prophets, and their conspiracy
theories are impoverished prophecies. Vaughan understands this even
as he embodies it. (It is a nice touch that one year prior Koteas had
played the lapsed priest in *The Prophecy,* saving the world from un-
imaginable atrocities.) Any emotional connection, or even the desire
for it, must be mediated through the violence of the machine, and
thus, again, through the physical. Cronenberg's vision of venereal
evolution is internalized to a state of altered consciousness. The very
processes of thought are taken over, but, typically, in a conjectural
flux, as with Vaughan's shifting parodies of systematic thought when
he talks with Ballard.

Here is a con man so seedy and demented he might make Dr.
Benway cringe, and yet he is the center of all activity in the film.
Throughout the film the interrelation of sex scenes and car action
scenes builds to the climactic crash, in which Vaughan goes over the
overpass rail while pursuing Ballard and Catherine—a sort of homicidal sacrifice. After his death the characters translate his presence,
the force of his twisted charisma, to the car he drove and crashed in,
so that Vaughan succeeds, obliquely, in the fusion of body and machine.

Cronenberg points out,

> One of our touchstones for reality is our bodies. And yet they
> too are by definition ephemeral. So to whatever degree we cen-
> tre our reality—and our understanding of reality—in our bod-
> ies, we are surrendering that sense of reality to our bodies'
> ephemerality. That's maybe a connection between *Naked Lunch,
> Dead Ringers* and *Videodrome.* By affecting the body—whether
> it's with TV, drugs (invented or otherwise)—you alter your real-
> ity. (cited in Rodley, 1992: 145)

Given these remarks, *eXistenZ* is a culmination of Cronenberg's numerous obsessions, interests, and cautionary messages. Between *X*
and *Z* lies *Y,* which is the big question Cronenberg likes to ask, revealing not just his spirit of scientific inquiry, but the influence of Burroughs and Ballard in pushing something to an imaginative conclusion.

This original screenplay by Cronenberg begins in his typical demonstration fashion, in this instance of a seminar to try out a new vir-

tual reality game. Allegra Geller (Jennifer Jason Leigh), whose first name sets viewers up for the pace of the film, has designed the software for a new game played by using a metaflesh game pod that plugs into a "bioport" that the player has installed at the base of his or her spine. The pod, the color of which suggests internal organs, is "grown from fertilized amphibian eggs stuffed with synthetic DNA," a character later explains, building on the amphibian motif that runs throughout the film, from the two-headed lizard first spotted at a country gas station to the amphibian farm Allegra's coplayer Ted Pikul (Jude Law) "works" at when playing the game. The bioport looks rather like a sphincter, and the cord that plugs into it resembles entrails, or perhaps an umbilical cord. The concept is a state-of-the-art fusion of human and "machine," a cutting edge *Videodrome* situation. Other blends appear in the film: At the seminar, Allegra is wounded by someone using an organic gun that shoots human teeth as bullets; later in the movie, Pikul will fabricate a similar weapon out of the bones and viscera served up as "the Special" in a Chinese restaurant. Truly, Cronenberg's visuals in *eXistenZ* create a new level of squeamishness in the viewer.

The word *eXistenZ* functions in several ways, suggesting ecstasy as much as the questioning of existence that is the overarching theme of the film. Allegra is a very sensual character, caressing her game pod, draping its cord across her eyes and face, licking her finger and inserting it into Pikul's virginal game port after explaining, "New ports are sometimes a bit tight." This is a movie about fertility, abounding in sexual, womb, and genital imagery that is reinforced by the dialogue. *eXistenZ* is referred to as Allegra's baby, and the insertion procedure whereby an auto mechanic fits Pikul with his port seems like a birthing: Pikul's legs are temporarily paralyzed, as with an epidural; and the mechanic washes up like a doctor, even though the insertion is done with a gunlike machine and his hands do not need to be sterilized. During Pikul's first game experience, Allegra accuses him of "blowing" her pod and trapping the game software within it because he surged. "I didn't feel any surging!" Pikul says in panicky defense. Later, while playing the game, Pikul tongues Allegra's bioport, explaining afterward that it was not he, but his game character acting, which begins a steamy encounter that nearly leads to intercourse. But Pikul, who had resisted having a port installed as long as he did because he had "a phobia about being fitted" with one and preferred to retain a normal human body, halts their progress toward virtual sex. "I'm very worried about my body," he declares. "Where are our real bodies? Are they all right? What if they're hungry, what if there's danger? I feel really vulnerable. Disembodied."

Here Cronenberg is developing his key theme about existence and reality. Pikul wants to pause the game, observing, "I'm feeling a little disconnected from my real life. Kind of losing touch with the texture of it. D'you know what I mean? I actually think there's an element of psychosis involved here." Allegra takes this as good news, a sign that his central nervous system "is fully engaged with the game architecture." When Pikul does pause the game, he finds his real life seems unreal, that it feels like a game and he feels like a game character. Resuming the game, he and Allegra are taken to be members of the Realist Underground, a movement bent on destroying virtual reality games. Further complications come when a game character reveals himself to be a double agent working to subvert rather than uphold the realist cause, telling them that a Chinese waiter Pikul had killed was their contact, not himself. By this point, Pikul questions even whether Allegra is the real Allegra or a game character.

eXistenZ is the most playful of all Cronenberg's movies; it abounds in allusions to his oeuvre and to his influences. The most amusing example comes when Allegra and Pikul are holed up in a hotel; a fast-food bag on the table between them bears the name "Perky Pat's." In Philip K. Dick's seminal 1964 novel *The Three Stigmata of Palmer Eldritch,* Perky Pat is a Barbie-type figure complete with a sort of dreamhouse. By taking a drug called Can-D, stimulus-deprived Martian colonists can enter Perky Pat's world and frolic in a (more or less) guilt-free alternate reality. That Cronenberg put the name on a fast-food bag makes the joke doubly meaningful, given Dick's fascination with California junk culture. At times in *eXistenZ,* Cronenberg seems to be poking fun at both audience expectations and his own epistemological obsessions.

Cronenberg launches viewers into an additional favorite theme of his by having Allegra port into a sickly pod that releases thousands of spores intended to infect and kill game pods. When, ostensibly, they return to reality, the disease apparently has returned with Allegra and Pikul; she gives her pod a shot to fight infection and save her game program. "How can a game event come into real life?" Pikul wonders, leading to a humorous—for the viewer—exchange between the two when Allegra tells him he received an infected port. Referring to the diseased pod, she laments, "The poor thing was trying to tell us it was sick by introducing the theme of disease into the game," evoking Pikul's outburst, "The *theme* of disease? I'm fucking really infected!"

The sudden appearance of a game character leads Pikul to deduce they are still inside the game and to observe, "Something's slipped over the edge here, Allegra. Something's all wrong." And indeed it is. Allegra shoots what she declares to be a game character, but whom viewers have been led to believe was a real person. She then blows up Pikul, using a remote control to activate a bomb she had inserted into his port, claiming it was a plug to halt the infection. Cronenberg cuts to the game seminar with which he opened the film and to Allegra asking excitedly, "Have I won? Have I won the game?" Viewers recognize that all the game characters are sitting with her as human coplayers, and discover that Allegra is not the designer of eXistenZ, only ambitious to become a premiere game designer; the designer of eXistenZ had played the role of the double agent in the game. Just as a realist had tried to kill Allegra in the opening scene, Allegra and Pikul now turn on the game designer, saying he should suffer for the harm he has done to the human race in achieving "the most effective deforming of reality." After they kill him, they turn their guns on the man who had played the Chinese waiter in the game, who protests, "No, you don't have to shoot me! Hey, tell me the truth, are we still in the game?" Allegra, Pikul, and the other characters visible in the background are completely still, immobile. Thus ends the film. Cronenberg has offered the ultimate box-within-a-box puzzle. A rule in playing eXistenZ is that if a player does not say the right line to move the game forward, the game characters go into a loop, not responding verbally or moving significantly. Is the Chinese man the real player of the game? He is the only one moving and speaking; no one responds to his query. It would seem that he hasn't said the right line to move the game forward.

The mechanic who had inserted Michael's first bioport (perhaps not uncoincidentally played by Willem Dafoe, who had played Christ in Martin Scorsese's *The Last Temptation of Christ* [1988]) had asked him, regarding Allegra's previous game designs, "Did you ever play her game ArtGod? One word: capital A, capital G. . . . Thou, the player of the game ArtGod. Very spiritual. Funny too." This is Cronenberg's existential attitude. You create God; you can be your own god. Whatever you create, suffer through, flourish in—you shape your own world.

All of Cronenberg's major films end with death and/or catastrophe. Death is the ultimate closure. Given the hermetic quality of these films, this seems fitting, if at times constraining. Perhaps the most important element in Cronenberg's oeuvre, and the one that some people find the most distasteful, is the insistence that these deaths affirm rather than negate. Whether tragic, as is Brundle's, or genuinely absurd, as is Vaughan's, they invoke an apotheosis of the characters' complex drives, or at least of their narrative trajectories. We are using "apotheosis" here in its looser, more modern sense, but the term has a certain resonance, given the complexity of Cronenberg's fundamentally atheistic worldview. By altering being, or allowing it to be altered, humans might create a state of grace, even of transcendence. Yet the metaphysical remains rooted in the physical. As Cronenberg has said,

> I don't think that the flesh is necessarily treacherous, evil, bad. It is cantankerous, and it is independent. . . . It really is like colonialism. . . . Ultimately, [that independence] can be seen as the separation of a partner that could be very valuable as an equal rather than as something you dominate. I think that the flesh in my films is like that. (cited in Rodley, 1992: 80)

Chapter 5

The Apartment As a Cell of Horror

The idea that terrible things might be occurring in an adjacent dwelling, with only thin walls separating sanity from insanity, is very tantalizing in a frightening way. More than that, it provides filmmakers with a perfect model by which to explore the connections among, the interstices of, voyeurism, paranoia, and alienation. This basic concept can be played out with endless variations. The courtyard in Alfred Hitchcock's *Rear Window* forms a public arena, while the invalid photographer's imposed isolation makes for a desperate struggle against increasing interiority—and his voyeuristic spying on neighbors creates constant tension between the two states. A look at three films by Roman Polanski—*Repulsion, Rosemary's Baby,* and *The Tenant*—will reveal an obsessive pattern of interiority, enriched by certain details and motifs that carry across many of the director's films. David Cronenberg's *Shivers* is a reversal of that pattern, with all the occupants of a high-rise ultimately invading the society outside the building. *Eraserhead* and *Blue Velvet,* directed by David Lynch, provide the opportunity to discuss the character of the apartment dweller in yet other ways, in terms of the levels of engagement in various buildings. The protagonist of the first film is beset by neighbors and alternate realities emanating from within the apartment; the central female character of the second seems to live in a building devoid of other tenants, which emphasizes the internal/external nature of her crisis.

Although technically a suspense film, Alfred Hitchcock's *Rear Window* serves as the cornerstone of the subgenre of apartment horror for its queasy balance of perverse impulses and noble attributes, its depiction of voyeurism resulting as much from need as from desire. Gerald Mast describes the film in a way that brings out some of the key themes dealt with in movies of the apartment subgenre: "Hitchcock examines the thin line between fantasy and reality, perversion and normalcy, vice and virtue" (1976: 330). Voyeurism is introduced right from the start as the bored L. B. "Jeff" Jeffries (James Stewart), a photographer laid up with a broken leg, observes his neighbors in their apartments around a courtyard. A couple is sleeping on their fire escape because the temperature is in the nineties; a dancer whom Jeff dubs "Miss Torso" is putting on her bra. Viewers see only what Jeff sees. Hitchcock makes the audience complicit in the voyeurism and thus reprimanded by Jeff's physical therapist, Stella (Thelma Ritter), who remarks, "We've become a race of Peeping Toms. What people ought to do is get outside their own house and look in for a change." She warns him he will see things he should not, to which he responds he would welcome trouble. Jeff gets it in spades when he realizes the occupant of the apartment straight across from him has murdered his wife—and gotten away with it, so far.

Jeff initially uses binoculars to spy on the killer, Thorwald (Raymond Burr), but he clearly feels guilty about this and switches to his camera and a telescopic lens. Using the tools of his trade legitimates voyeurism for him. His girlfriend, Lisa (Grace Kelly), does not care for this hobby of spying on neighbors, calling it "diseased." She always turns on all the lights when she enters the apartment to prevent their seeing out. This move puts *them* on display, and in one of the eeriest shots in the movie Hitchcock has Thorwald sitting in his unlit living room, only the glow of his cigar visible in the darkness. Is he looking across at Jeff?

Listening to Jeff's murder theory, a detective friend questions his ability to explain everything he sees in other people's apartments: "That's a secret, private world you're looking into out there. People do a lot of things in private they couldn't possibly explain in public. . . . I wonder if it's ethical to watch a man with binoculars and a long focus lens?" Jeff retorts, "Do you suppose it's ethical even if you prove he didn't commit a crime?" The detective ends the debate by saying he is not much on rear-window ethics, but Hitchcock keeps viewers contemplating the issue. At one point, Jeff's spying on his neighbors might have put him in the position of being able to save a tenant he has named "Miss Lonelyhearts" from committing suicide, had she gone through with swallowing the sleeping pills he saw her contemplate.

Hitchcock includes a characteristic element of the paranoiac-thriller genre: the murder of a family pet. The killing was of another apartment dweller's dog, which was digging furiously in a courtyard flowerbed where Thorwald might have buried some evidence of the murder. Thorwald is the only tenant who did not come to the window when the owner bewailed the dog's death, and a photograph Jeff took two weeks earlier shows that the zinnias planted where the dog was digging are now shorter. This gives Jeff and the now-invested Lisa the justification they need for her to break into Thorwald's apartment to look for evidence. Hitchcock triumphantly pushes the voyeur obsession when Jeff, unable to leave his wheelchair, let alone his apartment, is forced to watch Thorwald return home and attack the snooping Lisa. He calls the police to save her, but, oddly, does not mention that he suspects Thorwald of murdering his wife.

With Lisa removed from danger because she has been arrested for breaking and entering, the danger shifts when Thorwald comes for the trapped photographer. Jeff turns to his camera equipment again, this time as a defense, and the theme of voyeurism gets different play when Jeff uses flashbulbs to momentarily blind the intruder in *his* apartment. Jeff is saved by the police, but not before Thorwald pushes him out of the window that has served as his visual exit from the apartment, ironically incurring a second broken leg that guarantees he will remain holed up in his apartment for some time to come.

Roman Polanski's *Repulsion* narrows gradually from the outside world to demented interior, mirroring the mental disintegration of the central character, Carole (Catherine Deneuve), a manicurist whose nervous habit of biting her nails will become, in retrospect, a significant oral fixation rather than an amusingly ironic personal habit. The opening shot, a close-up of a blinking eye, will be associated with the inscrutable expression Carole wears in a family photograph. The photo is more of a question than an explanation of this character, emphasizing that insanity can never be explained away.

The first time viewers see the inside of the apartment Carole shares with her sister Hélène (Yvonne Furneaux) they get a foot-level view of a bolt on the apartment door and become aware there is a peephole for screening potential visitors. Such locks, barricades, and peepholes work through all of Polanski's apartment films. They cannot keep sound out, however, and in *Repulsion* the bell from the convent next door, a neighbor with her dog, the elevator, and someone practicing piano scales are heard. Indeed, an important aspect of most apartment horror films is the bleeding through of sound from adjacent dwellings. Most intrusive here, though, are the sounds that originate within the apartment: Hélène having sex with her married boyfriend, Michael (Ian Hendry). Despite the wardrobe in front of the door between the two bedrooms, Carole cannot avoid listening to this encounter; the noise comes through the door, through the fireplace, through the very walls of her room. (It is worth noting that the short film Polanski made in his third year at the State Film School in Lodz is titled *Two Men and a Wardrobe* [1958]; this piece of furniture figures in several of his works.) Carole's continual brush-off of would-be suitor Colin (John Fraser) is thus explained: While using Hélène's hair brush, Carole looks at the sheets where the couple had sex and obviously feels contaminated. Male sexuality intrudes on her space, which she is desperately trying to preserve. At work a friend tells the tale of a brutal boyfriend, street workers wolf-call as Carole walks by, and when Colin kisses her she wipes her mouth and rushes into her apartment to brush her teeth. Even Michael's toothbrush and shaving things are in her way in the bathroom. This disgust escalates until she hallucinates that the door behind the wardrobe opens and a hairy, grotesque man, looking rather like one of the street workers, comes into her bedroom and rapes her.

When Hélène and Michael go on holiday, Polanski piles up the symbols of Carole's severing from reality. The uncooked, putrid, fetallike skinned rabbit that had once been destined for Hélène and Michael's dinner becomes a key image, even making an appearance in Carole's purse at work. Carole sleeps a lot; she childishly eats sugar cubes; she looks at the family photo and the wall cracks behind it; as she touches the wall, it turns soft and retains the imprint of her fingers. She has fugues, psychotic episodes when she loses her sense of self and freezes while staring at something, as she did in the opening scene with a client's hand. Finally, she can no longer leave the apartment.

When a worried Colin arrives, breaks open the outer door of the apartment, and shuts it to prevent the neighbor with the dog from staring at them, Carole bludgeons him to death with a candlestick, then uses it as a hammer to barricade the door. She places Colin's body in the bathtub, filled with purifying water, but the threat of male sexuality cannot be removed or kept out, for she hallucinates another rape. Polanski escalates the expressionism, causing the rooms of the apartment to expand in length and size, intensifying the light/dark contrast, and depicting the hallway walls cracking open to admit hands that grab at and grope Carole. Her hallucinations nearly turn into reality when the lecherous landlord lets himself into the apartment, seeking overdue rent but now thinking about taking payment in kind, despite the putrid atmosphere. Carole slashes him to death with Michael's razor.

After the second murder, Carole irons Michael's dirty undershirt (a garment which had caused her to vomit before) with an unplugged iron and puts on her sister's lipstick like a child would, as if she is playing at Michael being her boyfriend. Perhaps as punishment for this vicarious fulfillment she has another rape hallucination, which pushes her completely over the edge: Groping hands again protrude from the hallway walls, and while she is lying prone on the bed, the ceiling descends on her terrified eye. When Michael and Hélène return they find Carole under her bed, sunk completely into madness. Heretofore aloof neighbors crowd into the apartment to help, but Michael will not let anyone else touch her. As he picks her up and carries her limp, completely vulnerable body, the expression Michael casts upon Carole's face is inscrutable. Polanski's final shot is of the family photograph. The camera moves in on the young Carole's face, into her still eye, a reversal of his opening move outward from the blinking eye.

Repulsion was Polanski's original screenplay and arguably his best apartment film. Yet he does infuse his film adaptations of others' stories with his own obsessions about space, sexuality, and intrusion. In fact, he obviously chose his sources with an eye toward developing those obsessions. *Rosemary's Baby,* based on Ira Levin's 1967 novel, focuses on a New York City apartment building called the Bramford, which has nineteenth-century Gothic architectural details and a dark clientele to match. Tenants have ranged from witches to cannibals to Satanists, and soon will include an actor who apparently has never read *Faust.* While Guy (John Cassavetes) and his wife Rosemary (Mia Farrow) tour the apartment left vacant by an old woman who *didn't* die in it, as the superintendent assures them, Polanski again lets the sound of someone practicing piano scales bleed through the walls, soon tumbling into *Für Elise,* the tender melody heard in the background during numerous scenes. Neighbors, the Castevets (Sidney Blackmer and Ruth Gordon), appear to be a dotty old couple, but while first visiting their apartment, Rosemary observes that they have removed pictures from their walls, which viewers later learn included the portrait of Roman Castevet's evil father, Adrian Marcato. Guy is taken in by Roman's stories of travel and adventure, and visits the Castevets the following night without Rosemary. Shortly thereafter he gets a choice role because a rival actor suddenly and inexplicably goes blind. Guy has sold his soul *and* his wife: Rosemary is to be the replacement for a woman the Castevets had taken off the street to cultivate as the receptacle for Satan's seed but who killed herself by jumping from their seventh-floor apartment window. One night, after eating Minnie Castevet's special "mouse," as she pronounces *mousse,* a drugged Rosemary is raped by the devil.

The further she progresses in her pregnancy, the more Rosemary wants to stay at home, alone, in the apartment. At one point Roman asks her, "Do you need anything from outside?" Rosemary's friend Hutch expresses concern when he asks, "Do you go out at all?" He urges her to meet him at the ironically appropriate Time and Life Building but does not show up—he falls into a coma, another victim of the witches' evildoing. After Rosemary's final excursion outside to her former obstetrician, who returns her to the evil Dr. Sapirstein (Ralph Bellamy) the Castevets and Guy had insisted she see, Rosemary locks herself in the apartment—but not before Guy's hand reaches through the partly closed door and tries to grab her, a typical Polanski touch. While much of this sequestering must be credited to Levin, one can see why Polanski was drawn to creating a film from the novel. It is full of images that fascinate him, such as a chest of drawers before a closet containing a hidden passageway to the Castevets' apartment. After Rosemary bolts herself in, Dr. Sapirstein and the others enter the apartment effortlessly through this passageway and use force to sedate her. Like the groping hands, the hypodermic needle is a recurrent image in Polanski's movies.

Rosemary is drugged often during her residency in the apartment building, but she resists it from the start, eating only a bit of the mousse, refusing the herbal beverages Minnie concocts for her, and hiding rather than swallowing the sleeping pills she is given after the birth of her child. In this way she tries to retain mental clarity to save herself and her baby, and ultimately she does, in a sense, for her maternal instinct leads her to willingly remain in the apartment building to nurse the demon infant. The implication, of course, is that this evil will at some point emerge from the apartment to wreak havoc on the world.

For the lesser yet oddly compelling film *The Tenant,* Polanski himself acts the lead role of a young man, Trelkovsky, seeking an apartment in Paris. Shots of the apartment building's courtyard and an ascension up a vertiginous staircase owe their debt to Hitchcock, being expansive yet claustrophobic at the same time. The motif of barricaded doors—which does not appear in Roland Topor's 1966 French novel of the same title—is set immediately by the actions of the concierge (Shelley Winters), who orders Trelkovsky to close her apartment's half door and who locks it when she takes him to see the vacant apartment, the door of which has multiple locks. The former tenant, Simone, had jumped out of the window (Polanski seems drawn to defenestration) and dies shortly after Trelkovsky takes her apartment, which still contains her personal belongings. Trelkovsky had visited Simone in the hospital and attends her funeral, listening to the preacher declaim on carnality and threaten those gathered, "The graveyard is where you belong."

From a window in his apartment Trelkovsky can see into the communal bathroom across the courtyard—the concierge had practically invited him to peep by noting, "It's a view worth looking at." At first he observes a neighbor using the facilities routinely, but soon the occupants seem to be staring back at him, and they appear as still as a photograph. At one point he uses binoculars to look at a man who, with his arms crossed, is looking back at him. He tells a co-worker that these people stand there for hours.

This visual element of creepiness is offset by the way sound becomes a joke in this film. Before moving in, Trelkovsky is warned that the landlord and his wife do not like noise, and he is threatened with eviction after having friends over. One time he returns home to find the apartment has been ransacked, throws a shoe in anger, and the neighbors respond by pounding on the walls. "You didn't notice noise when the thieves were here!" he yells in frustration. It is suggested that he wear slippers after ten o'clock at night, as had Simone: "It was much more comfortable for her—and for the neighbors," the landlord stresses.

This little suggestion feeds Trelkovsky's paranoia that all his neighbors are trying to turn him into Simone. The concierge gives him her mail. A café owner pushes her brand of cigarettes and choice of beverage on him. Eventually, he willingly smokes her brand—and ends up wearing her nail polish and clothes as well. From the hospital visit onward, Trelkovsky has kept up the pretense with Simone's friends that he too was her acquaintance, and at one point asks one of them, "At what precise moment does an individual stop being who he thinks he is?" Watching the repair of the skylight Simone had broken in her fall, he says to himself, "What happened to suicide? Well, I'll show them." Dressed in drag and wearing a wig, Trelkovsky sinks deeply into dementia as "Simone." He sees disembodied heads floating around the courtyard; a woman being forced into a jester outfit, the masque of which turns into his face; and a group of tenants coming after him. He barricades himself in his apartment by pushing a wardrobe (again!) in front of the door, and when a hand reaches in through the door's broken window and gropes for him, he stabs at it with a kitchen knife.

Even escape from his apartment offers Trelkovsky no relief. He goes to stay with a friend of Simone's, but after the woman leaves for work a salesman rings the doorbell, and Trelkovsky watches through the peephole as the stranger transforms into his landlord. He rents a hotel room, tries, unsuccessfully, to buy a gun to kill himself, and, fleeing the gun shop, is hit by a car. The innocent old couple that had been driving the car transform into the landlord and a nosy tenant as they are bending over him; a doctor on the scene gives Trelkovsky a shot to calm him down. Returned to his apartment building by the old couple, he knocks down the concierge to get back to his apartment, where he dresses in Simone's clothes. As Trelkovsky looks out into the courtyard, he envisions the windows of other apartments as theater boxes, he hears an orchestra warming up, and Polanski offers expressionistic shots of the neighbors applauding as "Simone" is about to jump from the window. In Topor's novel, whether Trelkovsky jumps or is pushed by other tenants is unclear. "Trelkovsky's body seesawed across the sill of his window" (1966: 179) and "For the second time, Trelkovsky's body seesawed across the window sill" (1966: 185) are the two phrases Topor uses to describe the action. Polanski invigorates the scenes to highlight the double defenestration: dressed in Simone's clothing, Trelkovsky clearly jumps out of his apartment window, drags himself painfully up several flights of stairs, and jumps out of his window again.

In effect, Polanski has built on Topor's novel to create a satire of the horrors depicted in *Repulsion* and *Rosemary's Baby.* Nosy or invasive neighbors become a conspiracy bent on driving a tenant to suicide. The normal sounds of everyday living are forced into silence by house rules. Madness erupts in the form of cross-dressing. Perhaps feeling as though he had worked the subgenre over, since making *The Tenant,* Polanski has not again dealt with the apartment as a vehicle of horror, although the theme of isolation and torture recur in later films such as *Death and the Maiden* (1994).

Shivers, David Cronenberg's first feature, takes an opposing tack to the other films of the apartment-horror subgenre. Rather than focusing on the increasing isolation and paranoia of a central character, Cronenberg shows an entire high-rise apartment building descending into polymorphously perverse insanity. In this it resembles J. G. Ballard's *High Rise* (1975), published the same year Cronenberg's film was released, except that Ballard depicts a group reduced to savagery through purely psychological causes—the isolation of the island apartment tower combined with mass neuroses and class divisions—whereas Cronenberg offers a quasi-scientific cause and effect that could be seen either as catastrophe or as major evolutionary development.

The story in its simplest form: Starliner Towers is a state-of-the-art, virtually self-sufficient high rise set on an island outside a major city infested by feceslike, wormlike parasites that causes the tenants to lose all rational control and plunge into an insatiable, brutal orgy (the original title for the film was *Orgy of the Blood Parasites*). As in many of his subsequent movies, here Cronenberg uses the horror genre to explore the nastier possibilities of human evolution in a framework that allows for the suspension of conventional morality. He notes that *Shivers* is "about repression and restriction, it tries to remove responsibility from the equation, and look at how certain more instinctive drives might work" (cited in Wells, 2000: 89). The spread of the "blood parasites" is never judged as evil; if anything, it is portrayed as an almost logical and inevitable expansion of human potential. This is the kind of fictional treatment that has made Cronenberg a highly controversial filmmaker. Besides Hitchcock, another master at exploring the beneficial effects of perversion, no other filmmaker of the subgenre has worked with such a large canvas and made questionable behavior so redeeming.

The basic premise is unsettling enough. Early in the film, viewers see Dr. Emil Hobbes (Fred Doederlein), the mad scientist who starts all the mayhem, strangle what appears to be a schoolgirl, tape her mouth shut, slit open her torso and pour acid into it, then slit his own throat. The girl, viewers discover, was Hobbes's mistress and failed medical experiment, and the tape was to prevent her internal parasites from escaping. Hobbes's colleague, Rollo Linski (Joe Silver), explains to Dr. Roger St. Luc (Paul Hampton), the house physician, that "Hobbes believed that man is . . . an overrational animal that's lost touch with its body and its instincts." Hobbes's solution was a parasite that would eat a human's failing organ and then function as the organ's replacement. It's a very practical notion, as Cronenberg has Linski present it: "You got man, right? And you've got parasites that live in, on, or around him, right? Why not breed a parasite that can do something useful? A parasite that can take over the function of a human organ . . ." The problem is, the parasites turn out to be "a combination of an aphrodisiac and venereal disease," and they cannot be controlled.

What distinguishes the movie, though, beyond that relatively novel concept, is the glee with which it attacks bourgeois morality and, ultimately, how essential that celebratory quality is to the film's success, at least on its own terms. Cronenberg himself gave a fair description of his intentions and their effect in an interview:

> The demon in *Shivers* is that people vicariously enjoy the scenes where guys kick down doors and do whatever they want to the people inside. They love the scenes where people are running, screaming, naked through the halls. But they might just hate themselves for liking them. This is no new process; it's obvious that there is a vicarious thrill involved in seeing the forbidden. (cited in Rodley, 1992: 50)

Cronenberg lets viewers come to know the cross-section of the Starliner Towers' population—the doorman, an insurance claims worker named Nicholas Tudor (Allan Migicovsky), St. Luc, and others—well enough to become involved in the horror, but not so well that viewers cannot enjoy the events with detachment.

Cronenberg offers equal amounts of gore and intelligence. Quite memorable is the scene in which Linski has Tudor's parasite on him and tries to rip it off and kill it with a pair of pliers. Tudor enters the room, grabs the parasite, swallows it, and kills Linski. Yet for all the graphic depictions of mutilation, murder, and parasitical rape, the scene that best illuminates the central thesis of *Shivers* is a relatively quiet conversation, showing that even at this early stage in his career Cronenberg had a gift for eloquently crystallizing his obsessions. St. Luc is talking with Nurse Forsythe (Lynn Lowry), who relates a dream she had in which a repulsive old man had told her that "Everything is sexual . . . even old flesh is erotic flesh. That disease is the love of two alien kinds of creatures for each other. That even dying is an act of eroticism." Then a parasite wriggles out of her mouth. St. Luc knocks her out with a punch, and he is the last to succumb, yet that submission and the following denouement, in which the highrise tenants all drive toward the mainland at daybreak, seem inevitable. With that ending, *Shivers* fulfills a key requirement of the apartment-horror subgenre, that the demented isolation of the dwelling space expand at some point to join, and most likely contaminate, the larger society surrounding it. This gives additional resonance to the title under which the film was released in the United States, *They Came from Within*.

As enraptured as *Shivers* is in its portrayal of mutating life, *Eraserhead* is riddled with fears and doubts. To call *Eraserhead* a "horror movie" is like calling cognac a sort of grape juice. David Lynch's first masterpiece, labored over for five years, is a nonlinear, surrealist exploration of themes and motifs common to a young father's anxieties, hopes, and desires. Nonetheless, it is the most truly horrifying of the films discussed here, and perhaps the purest in its focus on the apartment.

The larger setting, an industrial wasteland filled with clanking machinery and steam-belching ductwork, makes the apartment of the central character, Henry (Jack Nance), a sanctum from the enveloping claustrophobic environment, but he can keep the outer world from intruding only by retreating into smaller, more phantasmic worlds. This paradox shapes the movie. But to put the dynamic so concisely betrays Lynch's free-roaming, impressionistic approach. *Eraserhead* opens with an eerie montage sequence, introducing most of the visual elements that will be developed, including Henry's head floating (superimposed) in *space* (what he longs for), a planetoid that reveals a crevice in which a God-figure pulls gears and makes sparks (the grinding gears of fate), and, most important, a wormlike creature emerging from Henry's mouth. This creature drops into a puddle, and the viewer sinks with it into Henry's world.

Henry is going home to his sad little apartment room, carrying his pathetic bag of groceries—a reference to his maternal nature. He passes through an industrial landscape and over mounded terrain as if he were traversing the surface of another planet, both a hearkening back to the planetoid in the montage and a foreshadowing of the cheeks of the Lady in the Radiator (Laurel Near). When he gets home, he settles into his domestic routine by turning on an antiquated phonograph and checking over his cloistered, bachelor environment, an important part of which is the view from his sole window—the brick wall of the neighboring building. This seems to be an allusion to Herman Melville's short story "Bartleby, the Scrivener," about a Wall Street clerk who "prefers not to" execute tasks for his employer, spends his days staring at the brick wall of the building opposite, and ends up driving the lawyer from his rented offices because Bartleby has taken up residence in them. The story is a sad commentary on the lack of meaningful communication, and Lynch does well to associate such a loaded reference with Henry: ultimately, Henry cannot even see the brick wall, so clouded over has his window become.

While Henry seems resigned and lethargic at best, the room itself is striving for life. The carpet appears to be on the verge of writhing, the magnified view of its fibers bearing resemblance to mulch. There is a large mound of earth on the chest of drawers, and it appears to be covered with hairlike fibers. The radiator, its noises inseparable from those heard leaking in from outside the building, thrums and throbs with fertile possibilities. It waits expectantly.

The movie has two interwoven threads of thematic development: the entry of tortured, even mutilated, life into this toxic environment, and Henry's fragmented attempts to escape it. He is invited to dinner at the home of his girlfriend, Mary (Charlotte Stewart), where her parents serve miniature artificial chickens. When Henry tries to carve his, the bird's legs kick and blood oozes from its body cavity. A dog is suckling its litter of puppies, and Henry learns that Mary has given birth to his child. ("They're still not sure it is a baby," Mary qualifies.) He gets a nosebleed from this news, coupled with Mary's mother's insistence that the new parents wed, yet another of Lynch's visual allusions to the blood involved in birthing. Mary and offspring move in with Henry.

The "baby" is repellant and heartbreaking at the same time, a skin-less fetal creature whose apparently limbless torso is wrapped in a cloth bandage. This limblessness suggests a connection to the worm-like creatures that appear throughout the film. Viewers see Henry outside the apartment with a small grublike worm that he keeps in a little box; at home, he places it in an iconic cabinet that sits atop the chest of drawers. The baby's plaintive wailing drives Mary back to her parents' house, and the way she has to struggle to yank her suitcase out from under the bed is a comical and unsettling birthing image in its own right. With Mary gone, Henry takes on the roles of mother and nurse, taking the baby's temperature and providing it with a humidi-fier. As he sits by the infant, the brick wall outside looks as if it has gotten closer. The apartment's interior walls are dark. Whenever Henry tries to leave, the baby cries louder, hiccups, and gasps, then calms when Henry sits by it. Bound to the apartment by duty, Henry escapes by watching a woman with puffed, deformed cheeks—sug-gestive of the planetoid from the opening montage—do a bizarre stage routine inside the theater world of the radiator: Wormlike crea-tures drop from above her, and she smiles sheepishly as she stomps their heads into mush. Throughout most of the film, the soundtrack suggests erupting steam, connecting the radiator to the factories in Henry's neighborhood in a way that emphasizes his being enclosed, hemmed in.

The confinement of the single-room apartment emphasizes the travesty of domestic life at the heart of the film. Following the scene with the Lady in the Radiator, Henry wakes in bed to find that Mary has returned, and the scene manages both to encapsulate the movie's central issues and to connect them with the larger cosmic elements that seem to reign just beyond Henry's miserable, truncated exis-tence. Mary unfolds herself in a chrysalislike movement, fighting to get out of the sheet wrapped around her, and Henry finds umbilical, wormlike things in the bed that seem to have come out of her. He hurls them against the wall; they splat. The small grublike worm Henry had brought home now dances and enters a landscape like the planetoid seen in the opening sequence. It is likely Henry hallucinates this scene, including Mary's returning to him, for the woman who lives across the hall pays a visit and seduces him. The Lady in the Ra-diator sings, "In Heaven, everything is fine. You've got your good things and I've got mine," and Henry joins her onstage.

Henry next has a dream containing key images from the film: the God-like figure, blood, worms, the mound of dirt supporting a would-be tree that appears on Henry's bedside table, the baby's crying head. Henry's head pops off, falls into a puddle, and is snatched up by a street urchin, who takes it to a factory where it is made into erasers. It is more profitable to take these scenes as a rich medley of the film's themes than it is to analyze them as a dream, but nonetheless, dreaming that his head is made into pencil erasers indicates Henry's severe existential trauma.

Ultimately, Henry is left alone with the baby, which he kills in literally the most heart-rending euthanasia in cinematic history. This act breaks Henry's isolation, or seals it, depending on one's interpretation of the closing sequence. A storm seems to be raging outside, which Lynch links to the sound of the radiator. When Henry cuts open the baby's bandages, it appears to have neither skin nor internal organs in the usual sense, but Henry pierces what he takes to be its heart with a pair of scissors. The baby's neck extends, so that it becomes one of the omnipresent wormlike creatures, and its head appears to grow immense as it looms toward Henry. Lights surge and flash, then blank out. After a view of the God-figure from the opening scene, now struggling with the gears as sparks shoot up, Lynch provides a final, vaguely comforting glimpse of Henry dancing slowly with the Lady in the Radiator. Viewers are left with the question, Has he advanced or retreated, opened up or closed down?

Unlike *Eraserhead,* Lynch's *Blue Velvet* addresses the apartment fixation only tangentially, yet the apartment motif is vitally—or rather, stagnantly, given the main female character's situation—important. The film has an expansive view of alienation, an embracing grasp of paranoia. A man named Frank (Dennis Hopper) has kidnapped the husband and son of a lounge singer, Dorothy Valens (Isabella Rossellini), in order to extort her sexually. The young hero, Jeffrey Beaumont (Kyle MacLachlan), finding a severed and mouldering human ear in a field with ants crawling on it, stumbles into this situation and is drawn into the nightmarish underworld of his hometown, Lumberton. An earlier shot zooming in on beetles working away beneath the grass lets viewers know they are about to make a descent, and also reveals an insect motif, a comment on human behavior that Lynch shares with his surrealist filmmaker ancestors.

Blue Velvet shows how malleable the apartment horror subgenre is. As far as viewers are shown, despite the list of names on the building's directory and a lighted window here and there, Dorothy appears to be the sole resident of Deep River Apartments. Lynch evokes layers of meaning with this name, from "still waters run deep" to the song "Deep River," which contains a line about crossing over into Jordan; here the crossing is over into hell. Even the name of the street, Lincoln, implies the various sorts of slavery dealt with in this film. Dorothy survives alone and terrified. Her only human contact comes in frightening ways from outsiders, and ranges from Frank's brutality to Jeffrey's subtler, but equally unsettling, intrusions (ironically, he first gains entry to her apartment posing as a pest-control technician). The world can only ever be an outside attack, something for which she has to brace herself. Jeffrey, who learns that Dorothy's husband Don is missing, is keen on investigating whether the ear he found is Don's, speculating to a detective's daughter that one could learn a lot by sneaking into Dorothy's apartment and watching. The daughter, Sandy Williams (Laura Dern), a bit taken aback by Jeffrey's voyeuristic plan, later remarks, "I don't know if you're a detective or a pervert."

Lynch is notoriously reticent about the meaning or intent of his films, but Isabella Rossellini has given her own striking interpretation of the character she plays. For her, Dorothy was a battered woman who suffered, possibly, from Stockholm syndrome and tried to transcend her personal nightmare by creating a doll-like perfection in her appearance (Rodley, 1997). That interpretation is borne out by the way Dorothy lures Jeffrey into her suffering. Having stolen a key to the apartment during his first visit, Jeffrey lets himself in while Dorothy is at work—in her role as the Blue Lady singing "Blue Velvet" at the Slow Club lounge—and watches from the slatted living room closet as she undresses upon returning. He rattles a hanger; she ousts him while wielding a kitchen knife that rivals Norman Bates's and orders him to strip to his boxers. Pulling down the boxers, kneeling as if about to perform oral sex, Dorothy asks if he likes what she is doing, but Jeffrey's affirmative response is met with her reply of, "Don't touch me or I'll kill you! Do you like talk like that?"

Following that outburst, the sadistic Frank arrives, and viewers realize that Dorothy has been feebly attempting to imitate his gonzo brutality. He abuses her verbally and physically, raping and punching her. Although brutal to view, the scene is a key moment in the film's orchestration of concealment and disclosure, for Jeffrey watches it all through the slats of the closet door. Throughout the movie, much of his time in Dorothy's apartment is spent in the closet, which is clearly not a sexual-preference pun but rather an embodiment of an interior state: He uses the closet both for concealment and for voyeuristic observation. Dorothy and Jeffrey are isolated from each other when he is in the closet, most wrenchingly so during the rape, which puts viewers in mind of the connection between closets and abuse. Frank repeats "Mommy loves you" as he attacks Dorothy; "bad" children may be locked in a closet by an abusive parent, just as they might hide in a closet to avoid harm from that parent.

This isolated closet space underscores the relevance of the apartment in *Blue Velvet*. Purporting to be a crime thriller, it is actually a sort of fantasia rampant with shifting points of view, almost all of them interior, subjective, and even phantasmagoric. When Jeffrey or Frank enter Dorothy's apartment, they are in a way entering her psyche. On Jeffrey's subsequent visits, Dorothy tells him to hit her, that she wants him to hurt her, and although he does not want to, Jeffrey ends up striking her before they have sex. This is the behavior Frank has indoctrinated into Dorothy, and she can only replicate it with Jeffrey, pulling him further into the seedy underbelly of life in Lumberton: Frank, enraged at discovering Jeffrey's intimate relationship with Dorothy, abducts the young man, beats him up, and dumps him in the countryside.

Later, Sandy and Jeffrey's new relationship is tainted when a naked Dorothy turns up at Jeffrey's house, severely battered and in shock after a beating by Frank. Dorothy calls Jeffrey her secret lover and says to Sandy, "He put his disease in me"—a reference to Frank, but an allusion to Jeffrey's impure sexual state as well. Jeffrey finds the bodies of the murdered husband and a corrupt detective on what will be his last visit to Dorothy's apartment. Jeffrey's physical involvement with Dorothy spurred Frank to kill Don as punishment for her "infidelity" to Frank. The way Jeffrey gazes at the dead bodies and subsequently walks down the hallway upon leaving the apartment reveal how morally exhausted he is by this point. Then he is forced back into the apartment and the closet when Frank enters the building with a gun, and ends up having to shoot Frank point blank in the forehead to preserve his own life.

Lynch sustains the duality and moral ambiguity of that life throughout the film. Although Jeffrey wants to help Dorothy, he actually uses her and disposes of her. In stark contrast to Jeffrey's experiences and activities in Dorothy and Frank's world, Lynch shows him sipping Cokes through straws in a diner with Sandy as they discuss the missing person case and going to one of her high school friend's parties. At the end of the movie, the couple is surrounded by their loving families, preparing to have lunch on a sunny afternoon. A robin perches outside the Williams's kitchen window, a beetle struggling in its beak, an allusion to a dream Sandy had about robins that the two young people take as a good omen for their future. But for viewers that beetle hearkens back to the opening shot of insects mining away beneath the grass, a reminder of the dark underworld of Lumberton.

Lynch then visually contradicts what is going on in viewers' minds by providing a montage of idyllic small-town life that echoes his opening one: a fireman waving from a vintage red fire truck, white picket fences, flowers, a happy child toddling along. Lynch eases this last scene into a view of the now-widowed Dorothy by making that child be her released son, little Donnie. The two are alone in a park. Dorothy's expression, a look of loving tenderness for her son that shades into a look of fear and trauma, is the image Lynch leaves with viewers. She might be outdoors in a public space, but this is part of Lynch's expansive view of alienation. The abuse she suffered as the sole occupant of the apartment she had once shared with her nuclear family will torment and isolate Dorothy wherever she seeks asylum.

Many films of the apartment-horror subgenre deal with voyeurism. The need to connect, to be a part of the human cycle while staying isolated from the human throng has long been attributed to artists as a requirement for creativity. But it is clearly a larger human impulse as well. We want to see without being seen and to touch without being contaminated. Some of these films show how paranoia can develop from voyeurism as well as from isolation, and in extreme cases can lead to alienation, insanity, and death.

The films discussed in this chapter all contribute in various ways to demonstrate how voyeurism, paranoia, and isolation can shape and occasionally redeem, but more often destroy, human lives, and they do so by setting their exploration in that place called home, the apartment.

Chapter 6

Angels and Aliens: The Supernatural Other in Popular Consciousness

Since the late nineteenth century, angels and aliens have battled for supremacy in the popular imagination. Both are otherworldly creatures, assumed to be superior to their human counterparts—at least in terms of travel and ferocity—and equally capable of miracle and mayhem. In a word, irresistible. For most of the twentieth century, reflecting American cultural interest in space travel and the fear of nuclear annihilation, aliens seemed to be prevailing, as evidenced in movies ranging from *Invasion of the Body Snatchers* (1956) to *Alien* (1979) and its sequels, *Aliens* (1986), *Alien 3* (1992), and *Alien Resurrection* (1997). But at the turn of the millennium, angels became almost omnipresent in popular culture, manifesting in everything from mail-order catalogs to films such as the *Prophecy* trilogy. The *Prophecy* films link the two genres by representing angels as intergalactic intruders, making it apparent that an angel can be a destructive alien just as easily as an alien can be a saving angel—as Klaatu is, for example, in *The Day the Earth Stood Still*. Despite or because of its dubious aesthetic qualities, the first film in the *Prophecy* series provides a template for discussing the nexus of movies dealing with angels and aliens.

"Good" angels have long inhabited popular culture texts, serving as the vehicles of good deeds in such mainstream films as *It's a Wonderful Life* (1946) and *Michael* (1996). In *Nightmare on Main Street: Angels, Sadomasochism, and the Culture of Gothic* (1997), Mark Edmundson notes,

> Even the American clergy, generally receptive to any sign of awakening spirituality, views the angel craze askance. America's current angels are fluffy creatures. . . . In the Bible, they're

> beings of another order: an encounter with an angel transforms
> life—puts one on a harder, higher path. (80)

The *Prophecy* series is to be commended for restoring a more traditional depiction of angels as the harbingers of justice, even as great
pain and slaughter are strewn in their wake. The first film, *The Prophecy* (1995), written and directed by Gregory Widen, is the strongest,
the primary focus being on the interactions among angels Gabriel
(Christopher Walken) and Simon (Eric Stoltz); a former novitiate-
turned-cop, Thomas (Elias Koteas); and the fallen angel Lucifer
(Viggo Mortensen). Thomas lost his faith because he saw too much—
specifically, warring angels—and joined the police force seeking a
different outlet for his impulse to serve humanity. Saving humanity is
what he ends up assisting in: After Simon kills Gabriel's lieutenant,
Uziel, he swallows the evil soul of one Colonel Hawthorne so that
Gabriel will not get it. Hawthorne had been involved in human sacrifice during the Korean War, Widen's updating of Kurtz's crimes
against humanity in *Heart of Darkness,* so the already injured Simon
becomes increasingly sickened by the soul he is harboring. He passes
it to a child, aptly named Mary (Moriah Shining Dove Snyder).

What looms is a second angel war (although it is unclear whether
the first one ever really ended), with Gabriel wanting a return to the
way it was before the "monkeys"—humans—existed, a time when
God loved the angels best. These angels are not in the least reminiscent of the Hallmark card variety, which Thomas makes clear when
he expounds the following to Mary's teacher:

> Did you ever read the Bible, Katherine? Did you ever notice
> how in the Bible, whenever God needed to punish someone, or
> make an example, or whenever God needed a killing, he sent an
> angel? Did you ever wonder what a creature like that must be
> like? A whole existence spent praising your God, but always
> with one wing dipped in blood. Would you ever really want to
> see an angel?

Appropriately, the only way to kill an angel is to rip out its heart,
which Gabriel does to Simon. Lucifer appears and explains to Kath-
erine (Virginia Madsen) that all human souls will remain in limbo
while this war between angels goes on and that Gabriel is attempting
to steal the bleakest soul—Hawthorne's—to fight for him. If Gabriel

wins, Heaven will open to him, although Lucifer predicts, "I know that this new heaven will be just another hell."

Mary sickens from harboring Hawthorne's evil soul. Her American Indian relatives and friends perform the Enemy Ghost Wave Ceremony to cleanse and heal her. Simultaneously, Lucifer tears out Gabriel's heart and Mary expels Hawthorne's soul, which is destroyed by a blast of light from heaven. Widen smartly leaves issues a bit murky at the end of the film. Thomas asks Lucifer, "I have my soul, and I have my faith. What do you have, angel?" "Leave the light on, Thomas," Lucifer replies, an allusion to an earlier conversation the two had about Thomas's childhood fear that the devil was under his bed—which Lucifer had been.

The Prophecy II (1998) was directed by Greg Spence (whose only prior directing experience had been *Children of the Corn IV* [1996]); he wrote the screenplay with assistance from Matt Greenberg. The film, which went straight to video for a variety of reasons, is nearly unwatchable. It breaks all the angel rules, not the least of which being that angels have no sexual organs: Viewers are invited to watch the "male" angel Danyael (Russell Wong) bedding the human Valerie (Jennifer Beals). This act serves as the entire premise for the plot as Gabriel (Walken) seeks the angelically impregnated Valerie in order to destroy the child because it would be a nephilim. This half-angel, half-human being would have both angelic powers and free will, not a desirable combination, and would end the angel wars by uniting the opposing sides. *The Prophecy 3: The Ascent* (2000), directed by Patrick Lussier—veteran staff member on numerous Wes Craven films— has a much better script (by Carl V. Dupré and Joel Soisson) than the second movie and refers to elements of the first one. It is definitely campy (witness the scene in which Gabriel revisits a diner from the first movie and is remembered by the waitress) but also has a philosophy. Gabriel (Walken again) has been condemned to mortality by God yet seems to enjoy the new experience. He serves as guardian to Danyael (Dave Buzzotta), the half-angel, half-human child who was yet unborn in *Prophecy II,* who is now a visionary pursuing the genocidal Pyriel (Scott Cleverdon). The conclusion wraps back nicely to the situation in the first *Prophecy* film in that Gabriel and Danyael go to the Midwest and, with the assistance of the now-grown Native American girl, Mary (played again, deftly, by Snyder), find where Pyriel will descend to earth and defeat him.

The interaction between humans and angels may be most extensive in *Dogma* (1999), a movie that ultimately sends the message that God favors humans over angels—odd consolation given the violence done to humans by the angels in this film. With direction and screenplay by Kevin Smith, the basic situation seems like a parody of Wim Wenders' *Wings of Desire* (1988). In that film the angels empathize with humans and share in their sorrow and pain in attempts to alleviate suffering. In contrast, *Dogma*'s angels alternately toy with and kill humans. The plot is densely constructed and plays loose and fast with Christian theology, but nonetheless is an important contribution to the conception of angels as supernatural others who are primarily looking out for themselves.

The film is a macabre blend of silly humor and truly horrifying events. In the opening scene, viewers witness three hockey-stick-wielding thugs viciously beat an elderly man on a New Jersey boardwalk and leave him for dead. The attack appears to be wanton. At the end of the film, it is revealed that God is a skeeball fanatic who takes human form once a month for a few days to play, and the old man is this month's embodiment. This functions as an important element of the movie and serves as a theme that overarches numerous angel and alien movies: the absence of God during human encounters with the supernatural other. In *Dogma,* God is rendered physically unconscious and cannot intervene in human or divine affairs, which allows much mayhem to occur.

Ironically, the violence comes about because the Angel of Death, Loki (Matt Damon), tells God he is laying down the sword because the angel Bartleby (Ben Affleck) convinced him he should not kill. God banishes the pair to Earth—to Wisconsin, of all places—where they take out their frustrations on the humans with whom they interact. Learning that a plenary indulgence (an indulgence in the Roman Catholic Church that remits in full a temporal punishment) will be given at a New Jersey church's centennial celebration, the two angels anticipate transubstantiating into human beings to take advantage of it and get back into heaven. Since God is missing, Metatron (Alan Rickman), who functions as the Voice of God, attempts to convince a human to thwart Loki and Bartleby. Bethany Sloane (Linda Fiorentino), the human chosen, is a descendant of Jesus' younger sibling and a doubting Catholic who works in an abortion clinic yet nonetheless attends Mass every Sunday. Ultimately she does succeed in her mission, but not before a lot of damage is done to earthlings. Loki convinces a nun that God does not exist, shoots an adulterer on a bus, and kills a boardroom full of executives, sinners all, save one pure woman, whom he lets live. Bartleby, long the pacifist, becomes enraged when he comes to the realization that, unlike himself, a servant of God whose love is demanded, humans have the free will to choose—while God loves humans regardless, and loves them more than angels. Unhinged, Bartleby snaps a guard's neck outside of the church he had hoped would be his portal back into heaven; flies high into the sky with humans and drops them to their death; and, after Loki's wings have been clipped, kills the now-humanized angel, his closest friend.

In addition to this barrage of angelic violence, Azrael, a former muse condemned to hell, works behind the scenes to remove obstacles from Loki and Bartleby's route to success because as a demon, he himself cannot transubstantiate to take advantage of the plenary indulgence. Azrael knows that if the two angels manage to get back into heaven through this loophole in God's law, basically reversing His decree, civilization—including the hell Azrael is trapped in—will be destroyed. And so he sends his three agents of terror to beat God into a coma, go after Bethany, and kill various other humans. Preceding each attack, the three tap their hockey sticks on the ground and glare at their intended victims, presenting a menacing image of inverted Divine wrath.

The film does overturn these dark scenes by ending happily. Bethany figures out where God is and revives Her. God then destroys Bartleby, raises the slaughtered humans to heaven, and causes the ostensibly barren Bethany to become impregnated with the next scion of God.

Kevin Smith has made other movies with the characters Jay and Silent Bob, who function as prophets to assist Bethany, and Bethany's pregnancy leaves an opening for a sequel to *Dogma,* but none has yet appeared, although it is not too difficult to envision what its elements would be. As with the *Prophecy* scenarios, various groupings of angels and humans would gather their forces and come into violent conflict with one another in attempts to destroy or save humanity, depending on their bent. The partial or total absence of God during the struggles and, thus far, the triumph of good largely thanks to humans feeds viewers' desire to believe that the destiny of the human race—

both before and after death—does lie within our control. This all-important issue of control is at the forefront in the spectrum of alien movies as well.

Before discussing them, however, it is worth noting that in addition to the numerous works of science fiction H. G. Wells produced—one of which will be discussed shortly—he wrote an 1895 novel titled *The Wonderful Visit* about an angel who passes into the human world while he is dreaming and subsequently befriends a vicar. The two discuss the reciprocity of the experience, with humans dreaming of a divine world, and the vicar muses, "[T]here may be any number of three dimensional universes packed side by side, and all dimly dreaming of one another. There may be world upon world, universe upon universe" (Wells, 1895: 26). No one but the vicar believes the angel is indeed an angel; most think he is a hunchback, because his wings make a mound under the vicar's borrowed suit jacket. Even the doctor who sees the unclothed wings attributes them to a genetic disorder. As the vicar remarks to the angel, "Only exceptional people appreciate the exceptional" (1895: 73). After years of ministering to worldly, unimaginative parishioners, he is wavering in his belief: "When I was ailing in my youth," he tells the angel, "I felt almost the assurance of vision that beneath this temporary phantasm world was the real world—the enduring world of the Life Everlasting. But now—" (1895: 84). Confused, the vicar ponders over the angel's constitution being "Terrestrial Angelic, Angelic Terrestrial . . . See-Saw" (1895: 193).

Slowly the vicar is awakened to the beauty of the "Wonderland" (1895: 212) his visitor comes from, even as the angel feels that "The iron of the world was entering into his soul" (1895: 194). During the little more than a week's time the angel is on earth, he "traveled so far on the road to humanity. All the length of his Visit he had been meeting more and more of the harshness and conflict of this world, and losing touch with the glorious altitudes of his own" (1895: 233). Ultimately, the angel whips a selfish, possessive man whose barbed wire harmed a child picking flowers, while screaming at him, "You bestial thing of pride and lies! You who have overshadowed the souls of other men. You shallow fool with your horses and dogs! To lift your face against any living thing! Learn! Learn! Learn!" (1895: 237). The man falls motionless, and the angel thinks (incorrectly) that he is dead, feeling "appalled . . . at this last and overwhelming proof of his encroaching humanity" (1895: 241). Although it is not quite a happy ending to the novel, the angel redeems himself by running into the vicar's burning house to save a servant girl to whom he had become attached, she having rushed back into the house out of the same sentiment to save the violin the angel had played so beautifully upon; the two ascend to the angel's world. A year later, the vicar dies, never having gotten over his encounter with the angel, albeit still hearing the angelic music that made him believe in a better place than earth.

Just as angel movies—whether depicting "good" or "bad" angels—and the angel book by Wells (who, curiously enough, was an atheist) show humans coming to self-awareness as a result of their encounters with angels, "it is through learning to relate to the alien that man has learned to study himself," George E. Slusser and Eric S. Rabkin observe in their introduction to *Aliens: The Anthropology of Science Fiction* (1987: vii). Benevolent aliens are as much a staple of mainstream movies as are good angels. *Close Encounters of the Third Kind* (1977), *E.T. the Extra-Terrestrial* (1982), and *Cocoon* (1985) brought friendly travelers from outer space to enrich the lives of Earth's inhabitants. In the horror genre, the alien visitor of *The Day the Earth Stood Still* has come to save—albeit through threat of annihilation—the people of Earth from destroying themselves and, by extension, the universe. The film, directed by Robert Wise, is one of the most intelligent of the genre. Although Klaatu (Michael Rennie) exits his spaceship and declares, "We have come to visit you in peace, and with good will," a soldier shoots him. Trained to act against violence, an eight-foot-tall robot named Gort destroys all human weapons at the scene. This is the first example of maintaining peace through superior firepower, a notion that will be explained by Klaatu at the end of the film.

Human stupidity is highlighted throughout the film, whether it be the lackadaisical guards who do not see Klaatu sneaking aboard his spaceship or the doctors who assume that since Klaatu's body is humanlike, his planet's atmosphere must be like that of earth. "I'm impatient with stupidity. My people have learned to live without it," Klaatu retorts when doctors tell him there is no possibility that all the earth's leaders would gather in one place to listen to his imperative message that their experiments in atomic energy threaten to escalate into the destruction of other planets. Klaatu performs a dramatic but not destructive demonstration to get people's attention: He neutralizes electricity all over the world for the same half hour. This greatly annoys U.S. officials, who decide he must be taken dead or alive. Worried over what Gort might do if he is injured or killed, Klaatu teaches a human confidant, Helen (Patricia Neal), a phrase that has become legendary in the world of science fiction: "Klaatu Barata Niktu."

Of course, Klaatu is killed, Helen repeats the phrase correctly, and Gort revives Klaatu's body long enough for him to speak to the world delegates who have gathered outside the spaceship. Klaatu's final speech reveals what has driven the plot:

> The universe grows smaller every day. And the threat of aggression by any group, anywhere, can no longer be tolerated. There must be security for all, or no one is secure. Now this does not mean giving up any freedom, except the freedom to act irresponsibly. Your ancestors knew this when they made laws to govern themselves, and hired policemen to enforce them. We of the other planets have long accepted this principle. We have an organization for the mutual protection of all planets, and for the complete elimination of aggression.

Thus robots such as Gort are given absolute power to preserve the peace, and the aliens are "free to pursue more profitable enterprises." Earth can be run as humans wish, but if human violence threatens to extend to other planets, earth will be "reduced to a burned-out cinder." Therefore, Klaatu puts forth, "Your choice is simple: Join us and live in peace, or pursue your present course and face obliteration."

As a film produced during the Cold War, *The Day the Earth Stood Still* sent an important sociopolitical message, albeit one little heeded. A similar theme was suggested by *The War of the Worlds* (1953), based on H. G. Wells's 1897 novel of the same title. Nuclear devastation, biological warfare—the tireless efforts of humans to stop the aliens was more than a scientific updating of the usual Wellsian demonstration of the instinct for survival. The belief was that the United States could prevail in these arenas when conventional weaponry, such as the tanks and airplanes destroyed by the Martians' heat rays, failed. But the movie retains the basic premise of the book in terms of alien-human strengths and weaknesses: The Martians destroy "the best of human scientific and moral resistance with contemptuous ease" and are "finally beaten not by human ingenuity, but by unseen bacteria" (Coren, 1993: 52).

Barré Lyndon's screenplay is set just after World War II, in California, where numerous UFO sightings had been reported in the early 1950s (Smith, 2002: 106). What appears to be a meteor crashes to the earth, but Dr. Clayton Forrester (Gene Barry), an astronuclear physicist, declares it is not. Three men are left to guard the cylindrical object overnight and, as in *The Day the Earth Stood Still,* humans make geocentric assumptions about aliens. The three think that those inside the cylinder will understand that a white flag means peace, and a pastor operates on the conviction that the visitors believe in Christian religions and understand English when he approaches their spaceship the next morning reading from the Psalms (that, or he is bucking up his own courage for an encounter with the Martians). The aliens quickly destroy these humans with heat rays, which comes as a surprise to the surviving humans. Forrester reasons about the aliens, "If they're mortal, they must have mortal weaknesses. They'll be stopped— somehow." When scientists analyze an alien "blood" sample, they are amazed at how anemic it is. One remarks, "They may be mental giants, but by our standards, physically, they must be very primitive."

Director Byron Haskin uses the narrative technique of gradually revealing, through flashes and glimpses, what the Martians look like, and viewers never get a sustained look at them. This method of gradual revelation would be used in later films such as *Alien* and *Fire in the Sky* (1993), although in both of those, as in most other later alien films, viewers are provided with a full, long look at the alien. This could be chalked up to advances in special effects, despite Albert Nozaki, under Hal Pereira's supervision, having put a great deal of thought and ingenuity into creating the Martian for *The War of the Worlds* (Smith, 2002). At the end of the film, when the spaceships crash into buildings and come to a grinding halt in the streets of a city because their pilots are dying, viewers are offered an image that could be interpreted several ways. The spaceship's door opens and a long, thin Martian arm reaches out, pulling itself along by its suction-cup tipped fingers. Is this an attempt to disembark and continue the battle one on one, Martian *a mano?* Is it the instinctual last gasp of a dying organism, or even a reach for sympathy?

No such questions arise with the titular creature in Ridley Scott's *Alien.* As one critic put it, the monster is "personified malignancy, pure and simple, with seemingly only one goal: to kill" (Paul, 1994: 390). It is, in a sense, the Angel of Death, the Exterminating Angel, the avenging linchpin in Judeo-Christian mythology, from Genesis to Revelation—which makes it all the more striking that the film's thematic elements, such as they are, emphasize embryosis, gestation, and release—in short, creation rather than destruction. This seeming paradox is made even more apt and sinister in the first movie, when the alien is asexual, of indeterminate gender. It was only in the second film of the series, *Aliens,* that the monster proved distinctly female.

The crew of the space-freighter Nostromo (screenplay writer Dan O'Bannon thus underscoring his theme of material versus moral interests by borrowing the title of Joseph Conrad's novel for the spaceship) awake from cryogenic suspension, a sort of reverse incubation. Panning shots through entryways hint at the horrors to come, but also project the idea of birth canals as portals to another reality. The groggy crew, whose clothing during suspension suggested diapers, assembles for sustenance and information. The ship's computer system is addressed as "Mother." Symbols both of fertility and eternity pile up in the deceptively simplistic narrative as crew members descend to a planet in answer to a supposed distress beacon. They find a spacecraft half-submerged in the ground, with the "limbs" reaching up, looking like anything from fallopian tubes to an inverted halo, or even the *ouroboros,* the myth of the eternal return represented by a serpent eating its own tail. These images begin commingling with images of a different sort when the crew members find a gigantic pilot figure that is petrified, yet regal—apparently an ossified Supreme Being.

The key premise of *Alien* is that the offspring of the dead God-figure will carry on its mission of destruction. One of them attaches itself to the face of a crewmember, Kane (John Hurt), and against the orders of Ripley (Sigourney Weaver), quarantine is broken to let Kane board the Nostromo. Once aboard, the crablike thing removes itself, scuttles around, and is killed. But the creature, while attached to his head, the center of cognition, had implanted its offspring in Kane's body. This leads to the movie's most notorious scene, when the nascent alien bursts from the man's chest, from the center of vitality, of life, suggesting that the Angel of Death comes from both within and without, an alliance both holy and unholy. The steel-toothed creature erupts with grace, making a bold exit/entrance, then scurries, limbless and sexless, out of its uterine environs into the veins and arteries of the Nostromo.

O'Bannon's screenplay owes a lot to *It! The Terror from Beyond Space* (1958), whose screenplay was by veteran science fiction writer Jay Bixby. In *It!* an alien gets aboard a spaceship and begins killing the crew one by one to feed on their blood. Suspenseful partial shots of the monster, the use of shadow, even the way the alien is ultimately expelled from the ship all find their way into *Alien*. Different, however, is the alien creature itself. In *Alien,* the android Ash (Ian Holm) has been programmed to "Bring back alien life form, all other priorities rescinded," which is why he puts the crew in peril by responding to orders given by Dallas (Tom Skerritt) from outside the spaceship rather than Ripley's, given from within, and why he prevents others from subsequently killing the alien. He tells them that the alien is unkillable. "You still don't know what you're dealing with, do you?" he asks them. "The perfect organism. Its structural perfection is matched only by its hostility," which, of course, the crew has been experiencing in the form of deadly attacks against them. Ash admires the alien's "purity," its instinct for survival that is "unclouded by conscience, remorse, or delusions of morality." This last line describes the Angel of Death, enacting its duty with no regard for anything else.

Alien, then, can be read as a hybrid of the angel and the alien genres, addressing all the issues taken up by either genre on its own. On the most basic level, there is the issue of bodily autonomy, of whether humans can withstand an invasion or resurrection of the body. For that matter, is there life after death or life beyond earth? Another issue is whether humans are in control of their personal and societal destiny. Is the Other a helper or a destroyer, and how can one be sure? The deepest issue might be whether humans are the chosen ones, the loved ones, either by God or by beings from outer space. Are they worth forgiving, or even saving?

These issues are further complicated in Robert Lieberman's *Fire in the Sky,* when an abductee's life is radically changed by his encounter with—and probing by—the aliens. He undergoes what amounts to a religious revelation and transformation, which effectively alienates him from the rest of humanity—if not permanently, at least devastatingly so for a period of time. It might well be the most sinister alien movie to date. Whereas the monster in *Alien* and the Martian invaders in *The War of the Worlds* are certainly destructive enough in terms of violence and the deaths they cause, the aliens in *Fire in the Sky* demonstrate a clinical interest in humans that leaves viewers shuddering. Gregory Benford has criticized the image of the benevolent alien in science fiction, explaining, "Friendliness is a human category. Describing aliens that way robs them of their true nature, domesticates the strange" (1987: 14). The "true nature" of *Fire in the Sky*'s aliens is unmasked, quite literally: The popular human conception of what aliens look like, with large slanty eyes and a pointed-chin skull shape, is merely their spacesuit.

As Benford observes, "the truly alien doesn't just disturb or educate, it breaks down reality, often fatally, for us" (1987: 23). This is the experience of Travis Walton, the abductee in *Fire in the Sky*, although he does not die. The film opens with a quote from Seneca, "Chance makes a plaything of a man's life." Indeed it does. The movie is based on a book titled *The Walton Experience*, which was first published in 1978 and reissued in 1996 under the title *Fire in the Sky: The Walton Experience*, in response to the movie's release. In the preface to the reissue, Walton explains how his adventurous, curious personality lay behind his desire to know more about the UFO he and his fellow workers saw (1996). Travis Walton's character in the film, along with the actor's depiction of him, presents a slightly different persona.

Travis (D. B. Sweeney) is a happy-go-lucky, naive young man who entertains a pipe dream about co-owning a motorcycle dealership with his best friend Mike (Robert Patrick) and marrying Mike's younger sister Dana. He consoles his friend—who is about to be evicted for not paying the mortgage and whose marriage is falling apart—by offering him a donut, truly believing it will make Mike feel better about his problems. He is the perfect capture for the aliens, whose ship hovers in the night sky when Travis, Mike, and the rest of their logging crew are coming down out of the White Mountains in Arizona after a long day's work. Travis insists that Mike stop their truck, bounds out, and walks toward the ship, smiling. Although the others call out to him to return to the truck, Travis is rapt with the idea of seeing a spaceship, but before long a white beam freezes him and throws him to the ground. The frightened crew convinces Mike that Travis is dead, so they drive away at breakneck speed, although Mike soon returns alone to search for him, fruitlessly.

The viewer, having seen the abduction, sides with the members of the logging crew and therefore against the authorities. The formal search for Travis conducted by the sheriff, with dogs and a line of men moving across the landscape, is shot with documentary-style camera work that appears to be an allusion to the closing scenes of *Night of the Living Dead.* The authorities, represented foremost by the called-in expert Lieutenant Frank Watters (James Garner), have the same matter-of-fact attitude that Romero's hold. In this instance, they do not believe in aliens and are convinced that the other crew-members murdered Travis, or perhaps one did and the rest are covering for him. After Travis returns, Lieutenant Watters seizes on the belief that it was a hoax, fabricated so that the crew could sell their story to the tabloids. (Interestingly, on the drive up to work the morning of the abduction, the youngest crew member had been reading *The Inquisitor,* a tabloid like those that publish alien stories as a staple.)

Travis turns up after five days, cowering naked outside of a lone country gas station one night after having mustered up the wherewithal to call Mike to come get him. The viewer then becomes closely aligned with Travis and vicariously experiences the abusive curiosity of humans who are obsessed with an interaction with aliens. So although Travis returns with the rain, ostensibly, if figuratively, putting out the fire in the sky, flashbacks of his abduction haunt him, most immediately when two "scientists" corner him in the gas station bathroom while shoving camera and microphone in his face and demanding to know all the details of his experience. On the window behind Travis viewers see the slimy trails left by slender alien fingers with small suction-cup tips; the invasive attack of the two men echoes for Travis now, and viewers in retrospect, the probing by the aliens. Once in the hospital, the medical examination he undergoes is yet another physical violation.

Indeed, everything Travis experiences after his return is invasive, including his family and friends pressing a welcome-home party on him. Crawling underneath the kitchen table in retreat from the crowd, a quivering Travis gets pancake syrup dripped on him, which evokes his full memory of the abduction. The syrup recalls the slime in the podlike cocoon that was Travis's cell aboard the alien spaceship, one cell among hundreds stacked up on many levels that circled an open central space. The image is Gothic, organic, and technological at the same time, like aspects of the ship Nostromo and other works by the artist H. R. Giger, who did the designs for *Alien*. Because *Fire in the Sky* is unique in its detailed scenes aboard the spaceship (which are not recounted this way in Walton's book), and because they so graphically convey the horror Travis undergoes, they are worth noting.

Breaking through a thin, latexlike cover and leaning out to gain a look, Travis tumbles out of his cell, holding with one hand to a tether suggestive of an umbilical cord because of its organic appearance. Gravity is quite light, and he is pulled back upward and into another human's cell—an abductee whose lower torso is a bloody cavity in which Travis' fingers become embedded; the partial man is still cognizant. Travis explores, whimpering as he encounters slime everywhere, and eventually drifts down into an arena to find the aliens' empty spacesuits. Unsuited, the aliens appear similar to hairless, wizened old men, yet with fetallike large heads out of proportion to their slender bodies. Their personality, such as it is, displays none of the qualities of benign sages or innocent babies, however. The noseless, clench-mouthed, cold-eyed beings roughly drag Travis to an operating room, rip off his clothing, and strap him to a table with a latexlike sheet. One eye is clamped open and his mouth is plugged; both eye and mouth are filled with slime. The last thing he sees is a tentacled instrument that descends from the ceiling and sends a probe into his eye, ostensibly into his brain.

Given this experience, the ending of *Fire in the Sky* is unfittingly sentimental. Travis visits the divorced and reclusive Mike some two-and-a-half years after the abduction. While Mike lives in isolation, Travis is happily married to Dana, doting on his child—named Mike—and anticipating the birth of a second. Travis takes Mike to visit the abduction site, and viewers wonder along with Mike, "Why'd you bring me here?" Travis forgives Mike for leaving him on the night of the abduction, and the two appear to rekindle their friendship. Travis seems implausibly well adjusted in his present life after his horrific encounter with the aliens.

As a glance at any of the supermarket tabloids shows, aliens and angels support various crackpot beliefs and delusions. But as the nuanced film *Fire in the Sky* demonstrates, such obsessions, when treated with a combination of subtlety and audacity, reveal the importance of the supernatural Other in both popular imagination and self discovery. Angel or alien, each figure, an archetypal shadow of ourselves, reflects the terror of our inner cosmos.

Appendix

Filmography

Alien (1979), Ridley Scott
Alien Resurrection (1997), Jean-Pierre Jeunet
Alien 3 (1992), David Fincher
Aliens (1986), James Cameron
Army of Darkness (1993), Sam Raimi
Batman (1989), Tim Burton
Big Sleep, The (1946), Howard Hawks
Birds, The (1963), Alfred Hitchcock
Blair Witch Project, The (1999), Daniel Myrick, Eduardo Sánchez
Blood Beach (1981), Jeffrey Bloom
Blood Feast (1963), Herschell Gordon Lewis
Blue Velvet (1986), David Lynch
Book of Shadows: Blair Witch 2 (2000), Joe Berlinger
Brood, The (1979), David Cronenberg
Children of the Corn IV (1996), Greg Spence
Close Encounters of the Third Kind (1977), Steven Spielberg
Cocoon (1985), Ron Howard
Copycat (1995), Jon Amiel
Crash (1996), David Cronenberg
Darkman (1990), Sam Raimi
Dawn of the Dead (1978), George A. Romero
Day of the Dead (1985), George A. Romero
Day the Earth Stood Still, The (1951), Robert Wise
Dead Ringers (1988), David Cronenberg
Death and the Maiden (1994), Roman Polanski
Desperate Living (1977), John Waters
Dial "M" for Murder (1954), Alfred Hitchcock
Dogma (1999), Kevin Smith
Dracula (1931), Tod Browning
Ed Gein (2000), Chuck Parello
Elephant Man, The (1980), David Lynch
Entr'acte (1924), René Clair and Francis Picabia

Eraserhead (1977), David Lynch
E.T. the Extra-Terrestrial (1982), Steven Spielberg
Evil Dead, The (1981), Sam Raimi
Evil Dead II: Dead by Dawn (1987), Sam Raimi
eXistenZ (1999), David Cronenberg
Female Trouble (1974), John Waters
Fire in the Sky (1993), Robert Lieberman
Fly, The (1986), David Cronenberg
For Love of the Game (1999), Sam Raimi
Frankenstein (1931), James Whale
Freaks (1932), Tod Browning
Frenzy (1972), Alfred Hitchcock
Gift, The (2000), Sam Raimi
Girl Was Young, The (1937), Alfred Hitchcock
Godfather Part III, The (1990), Francis Ford Coppola
Haunting, The (1963), Robert Wise
Hour of the Wolf (1968), Ingmar Bergman
Invasion of the Body Snatchers (1956), Don Siegel
It! The Terror from Beyond Space (1958), Edward L. Cahn
It's a Wonderful Life (1946), Frank Capra
It's Alive (1974), Larry Cohen
La Coquille et le Clergyman (1928), Antonin Artaud and Germaine Dulac
L'Âge d'or (1930), Luis Buñuel
Last Temptation of Christ, The (1988), Martin Scorsese
Le Sang d'un Poète (1930), Jean Cocteau
L'Étoile de Mer (1928), Man Ray
Lodger, The (1927), Alfred Hitchcock
M (1931), Fritz Lang
Marnie (1964), Alfred Hitchcock
Michael (1996), Nora Ephron
Multiple Maniacs (1970), John Waters
Naked Kiss, The (1964), Samuel Fuller
Naked Lunch (1991), David Cronenberg
Night of the Living Dead (1968), George A. Romero
North by Northwest (1959), Alfred Hitchcock
Nosferatu (1922), F.W. Murnau
People Under the Stairs, The (1991), Wes Craven
Pi (1998), Darren Aronofsky
Pink Flamingos (1972), John Waters
Prophecy, The (1995), Gregory Widen
Prophecy II, The (1998), Greg Spence
Prophecy 3: The Ascent, The (2000), Patrick Lussier

Psycho (1960), Alfred Hitchcock
Rabid (1977), David Cronenberg
Rear Window (1954), Alfred Hitchcock
Repulsion (1965), Roman Polanski
Requiem for a Dream (2000), Darren Aronofsky
Rope (1948), Alfred Hitchcock
Rosemary's Baby (1968), Roman Polanski
Sabotage (1936), Alfred Hitchcock
Saboteur (1942), Alfred Hitchcock
Scanners (1981), David Cronenberg
Shadow of a Doubt (1943), Alfred Hitchcock
She Freak (1967), David F. Friedman
Shivers (1975), David Cronenberg
Silence of the Lambs, The (1991), Jonathan Demme
Simple Plan, A (1998), Sam Raimi
Sinbad and the Eye of the Tiger (1977), Sam Wanamaker
Spellbound (1945), Alfred Hitchcock
Spider-Man (2002), Sam Raimi
Stalker (1979), Andrei Tarkovsky
Strangers on a Train (1951), Alfred Hitchcock
Suspiria (1977), Dario Argento
Tenant, The (1976), Roman Polanski
Texas Chainsaw Massacre, The (1974), Tobe Hooper
Them! (1954), Gordon Douglas
Topaz (1969), Alfred Hitchcock
Twilight Zone: The Movie (1983), Joe Dante, John Landis, George Miller, and Steven Spielberg
Twin Peaks: Fire Walk with Me (1992), David Lynch
Two Men and a Wardrobe (1958), Roman Polanski
2,000 Maniacs (1964), Herschell Gordon Lewis
Un Chien Andalou (1929), Luis Buñuel
Vertigo (1958), Alfred Hitchcock
Videodrome (1983), David Cronenberg
War of the Worlds, The (1953), Byron Haskin
White Heat (1949), Raoul Walsh
Wings of Desire (1988), Wim Wenders
Young and Innocent (1937), Alfred Hitchcock

Bibliography

Anobile, Richard J. (ed.) (1974). *Alfred Hitchcock's* Psycho. New York: Avon Books.

Auerbach, Nina (1995). *Our Vampires, Ourselves.* Chicago: University of Chicago Press.

Badley, Linda (1995). *Film, Horror, and the Body Fantastic.* Westport, CT: Greenwood Press.

Ballard, J.G. (1975). *High Rise.* New York: Carroll and Graf Publishers, Inc.

———. (1985). Introduction to the French Edition. *Crash* (pp. 1-6). New York: Vintage Books.

Barr, Charles (1999). *English Hitchcock.* Moffat, Scotland: Cameron and Hollis.

Baxter, John (1994). *Buñuel.* New York: Carroll and Graf Publishers, Inc.

Benford, Gregory (1987). Effing the Ineffable. In George E. Slusser and Eric S. Rabkin (eds.), *Aliens: The Anthropology of Science Fiction* (pp. 13-25). Carbondale: Southern Illinois University Press.

Benshoff, Harry M. (1997). *Monsters in the Closet.* Manchester: Manchester University Press.

Bloch, Robert (1959). *Psycho.* New York: Simon and Schuster.

Buñuel, Luis (1994). *My Last Breath,* translated by Abigail Israel. London: Vintage Books.

———. (2000). The Cinema. In Paul Hammond (ed. and trans.), *The Shadow and Its Shadow: Surrealist Writings on the Cinema,* Third Edition (pp. 112-116). San Francisco: City Lights Books.

Buñuel, Luis and Salvador Dalí (1994). *Un Chien Andalou.* London: Faber and Faber, Ltd.

Burroughs, William S. (1992). *Naked Lunch.* New York: Grove Press, Inc.

Campbell, Joseph (1949). *The Hero with a Thousand Faces.* New York: Pantheon Books.

Carroll, Noel (1990). *The Philosophy of Horror.* New York: Routledge.

Clover, Carol (1992). *Men, Women, and Chain Saws.* Princeton, NJ: Princeton University Press.

Conrad, Joseph (1950). *Heart of Darkness and The Secret Sharer.* New York: Doubleday and Company, Inc.

———. (1960). *Nostromo.* New York: Doubleday and Company, Inc.

Coren, Michael (1993). *The Invisible Man: The Life and Liberties of H.G. Wells.* New York: Atheneum.

Creed, Barbara (1993). *The Monstrous-Feminine.* New York: Routledge.

Cronenberg, David (1996). *Crash.* London: Faber and Faber Limited.

Dalí, Salvador (1993). *The Secret Life of Salvador Dalí,* translated by Haakon M. Chevalier. New York: Dover Books.

Derry, Charles (1977). *Dark Dreams.* South Brunswick: A.S. Barnes.

Dick, Philip K. (1991). *The Three Stigmata of Palmer Eldritch.* New York: Vintage Books.

Dika, Vera (1990). *Games of Terror: Friday the 13th and the Films of the Stalker Cycle.* Rutherford, NJ: Fairleigh Dickinson University Press.

Drummond, Phillip (1994). Introduction to *Un Chien Andalou,* by Luis Buñuel and Salvador Dalí. London: Faber and Faber, Ltd.

Edmundson, Mark (1997). *Nightmare on Main Street: Angels, Sadomasochism, and the Culture of Gothic.* Cambridge, MA: Harvard University Press.

Ellison, Harlan (1967). *I Have No Mouth and I Must Scream.* New York: Pyramid Books.

Finkelstein, Haim (1987). Dali and *Un Chien Andalou:* The Nature of a Collaboration. In Rudolph E. Kuenzli (ed.), *Dada and Surrealist Film* (pp. 128-141). New York: Willis Locker and Owens.

Freeland, Cynthia A. (2000). *The Naked and The Dead: Evil and the Appeal of Horror.* Boulder, CO: Westview Press.

Gazetas, Aristides (2000). *An Introduction to World Cinema.* Jefferson, NC: McFarland and Company, Inc.

Giannetti, Louis D. (1976). *Understanding Movies,* Second Edition. Englewood Cliffs, NJ: Prentice-Hall, Inc.

Grant, Barry Keith (ed.) (1996). *The Dread of Difference.* Austin: University of Texas Press.

Grey, Ian (2000). Last Exit to Brooklyn Leads to Emptiness. *Orlando Weekly* <http://www.rottentomatoes.com> Search: Requiem for a Dream.

Halberstam, Judith (1995). *Skin Shows.* Durham, NC: Duke University Press.

Harris, Robert A. and Michael S. Lasky (1993). *The Complete Films of Alfred Hitchcock.* New York: Citadel Press.

Hawkins, Joan (2000). *Cutting Edge: Art-Horror and the Horrific Avant-Garde.* Minneapolis: University of Minnesota Press.

Hawthorne, Nathaniel (1982). Rappaccini's Daughter. In Roy Harvey Pearce (ed.), *Hawthorne: Tales and Sketches* (pp. 975-1005). New York: The Library of America.

Highsmith, Patricia (2001). *Strangers on a Train.* New York: W.W. Norton and Company, Inc.

Hitchcock, Alfred (1995). Why I Am Afraid of the Dark. In Sidney Gottlieb (ed.), *Hitchcock on Hitchcock: Selected Writings and Interviews* (pp. 142-145). Berkeley: University of California Press.

Internet Movie Database (2003). <http://www.imdb.com> Search: Requiem for a Dream.

Ives, John G. (1992). *John Waters.* New York: Thunder's Mouth Press.

Jackson, Shirley (1959). *The Haunting of Hill House.* New York: Viking Press.

Kafka, Franz (1979). The Metamorphosis. In Erich Heller (ed.), *The Basic Kafka* (pp. 1-54). New York: Pocket Books.

Kiernan, Thomas (1980). *The Roman Polanski Story.* New York: Grove Press, Inc.

Konigsberg, Ira (1987). *The Complete Film Dictionary*. New York: New American Library.

Kovács, Steven (1980). *From Enchantment to Rage: The Story of Surrealist Cinema*. Rutherford, NJ: Fairleigh Dickinson University Press.

Kristeva, Julia (1980). *Powers of Horror*. Paris: Sevil.

Kuenzli, Rudolph E. (ed.) (1987). Introduction. *Dada and Surrealist Film* (pp. 1-12). New York: Willis Locker and Owens.

Lane, Anthony (1999). In Love with Fear: How the Master of Suspense Made Fetishists of Us All. *The New Yorker*, August 16, pp. 80-86.

Levin, Ira (1967). *Rosemary's Baby*. New York: Random House, Inc.

Lewis, Matthew G. (1952). *The Monk*. New York: Grove Press.

Lovecraft, H.P. (1927). History of the *Necronomicon*. <http://www.think-aboutit.com/misc/great_cthulhu.htm>

Lyons, Donald (1994). *Independent Visions: A Critical Introduction to Recent Independent American Film*. New York: Ballantine Books.

Mast, Gerald (1976). *A Short History of the Movies*. Indianapolis, IN: Bobbs-Merril Company, Inc.

Matthews, J.H. (1971). *Surrealism and Film*. Ann Arbor: The University of Michigan Press.

McCarty, John (ed.) (1994). *The Fearmakers: The Screen's Directorial Masters of Suspense and Terror*. New York: St. Martin's Press.

———. (1995). *The Sleaze Merchants: Adventures in Exploitation Filmmaking*. New York: St. Martin's Press.

McGilligan, Patrick (2003). *Alfred Hitchcock: A Life in Darkness and Light*. New York: Regan Books.

Mead, Rebecca (1998). Cheeze Whiz. *The New Yorker*, November 23, pp. 40-45.

Morris, Peter (1994). *David Cronenberg: A Delicate Balance*. Toronto: ECW Press.

Naremore, James (1973). *Filmguide to* Psycho. Bloomington: Indiana University Press.

O'Brien, Geoffrey (2002). *Castaways of the Image Planet: Movies, Show Business, Public Spectacle*. Washington, DC: Counterpoint.

Paul, William (1994). *Laughing Screaming: Modern Hollywood Terror and Comedy*. New York: Columbia University Press.

Polanski, Roman (1975). *Polanski: Three Film Scripts*. New York: Harper and Row.

Rodley, Chris (ed.) (1992). *Cronenberg on Cronenberg*. London: Faber and Faber, Ltd.

———. (1997). *Lynch on Lynch*. London: Faber and Faber, Ltd.

Romero, George A. (1974). Preface to *Night of the Living Dead*, by John Russo. New York: Warner Books.

Royer, Diana (2003). Cultural Concern with Death in Literature. In Clifton D. Bryant (ed.), *Handbook of Death and Dying*, Volume 2: *The Response to Death* (pp. 998-1007). Thousand Oaks, CA: Sage Publications.

Sade, Marquis de (1967). *120 Days of Sodom*, translated by Austryn Wainhouse and Richard Seaver. New York: Grove Press.

Selby, Hubert Jr. (2000). *Requiem for a Dream*. New York: Thunder's Mouth Press.

Simpson, Philip L. (2000). *Psycho Paths: Tracking the Serial Killer Through Contemporary American Film and Fiction.* Carbondale: Southern Illinois University Press.

Slusser, George E. and Eric S. Rabkin (eds.) (1987). *Aliens: The Anthropology of Science Fiction.* Carbondale: Southern Illinois University Press.

Smith, Don G. (2002). *H.G. Wells on Film: The Utopian Nightmare.* Jefferson, NC: McFarland and Company, Inc.

Smith, Susan (2000). *Hitchcock: Suspense, Humour and Tone.* London: British Film Institute Publishing.

Spoto, Donald (1983). *The Dark Side of Genius: The Life of Alfred Hitchcock.* Boston: Little, Brown and Company.

Topor, Roland (1966). *The Tenant,* translated by Francis K. Price. Garden City, NY: Doubleday and Company, Inc.

Truffaut, François (1985). *Hitchcock,* Revised Edition by Helen G. Scott. New York: Simon and Schuster, Inc.

Tudor, Andrew (1989). *Monsters and Mad Scientists.* New York: B. Blackwell.

Walker, Barbara G. (1983). *The Woman's Encyclopedia of Myths and Secrets.* San Francisco: Harper and Row.

Waller, Gregory A. (1986). *The Living and the Undead: From Bram Stoker's* Dracula *to Romero's* Dawn of the Dead. Urbana: University of Illinois Press.

Walton, Travis (1996). *Fire in the Sky: The Walton Experience.* New York: Marlowe and Company.

Waters, John (1995). *Shock Value: A Tasteful Book About Bad Taste.* New York: Thunder's Mouth Press.

Weiss, Allan S. (1987). Between the Sign of the Scorpion and the Sign of the Cross: *L'Âge d'or.* In Rudolph E. Kuenzli (ed.), *Dada and Surrealist Film* (pp. 159-175). New York: Willis Locker and Owens.

Weiss, Andrea (1992). *Vampires and Violets: Lesbians in the Cinema.* London: J. Cape.

Wells, H.G. (1895). *The Wonderful Visit.* New York: Macmillan and Company.

———. (2003). *The War of the Worlds,* edited by Martin A. Danahay. Peterborough, Ontario: Broadview Press, Ltd.

Wells, Paul (2000). *The Horror Genre: From Beelzebub to Blair Witch.* London: Wallflower Publishing, Ltd.

Wiater, Stanley (1992). *Dark Visions: Conversations with the Masters of the Horror Film.* New York: Avon Books.

Williams, Linda (1981). *Figures of Desire: A Theory and Analysis of Surrealist Film.* Berkeley: University of California Press.

Wood, Robin (1960). *Hitchcock's Films Revisited.* New York: Columbia University Press.

Wood, Robin and Richard Lippe (eds.) (1979). *American Nightmare: Essays on the Horror Film.* Toronto: Festival of Festivals.

Index

Order a copy of this book with this form or online at:
http://www.haworthpress.com/store/product.asp?sku=5347

THE SPECTACLE OF ISOLATION IN HORROR FILMS
Dark Parades

_____ in hardbound at $29.95 (ISBN-13: 978-0-7890-2263-9; ISBN-10: 0-7890-2263-X)

_____ in softbound at $14.95 (ISBN-13: 978-0-7890-2264-6; ISBN-10: 0-7890-2264-8)

Or order online and use special offer code HEC25 in the shopping cart.

COST OF BOOKS_____

POSTAGE & HANDLING_____
(US: $4.00 for first book & $1.50
for each additional book)
(Outside US: $5.00 for first book
& $2.00 for each additional book)

SUBTOTAL_____

IN CANADA: ADD 7% GST_____

STATE TAX_____
(NJ, NY, OH, MN, CA, IL, IN, PA, & SD
residents, add appropriate local sales tax)

FINAL TOTAL_____
(If paying in Canadian funds,
convert using the current
exchange rate, UNESCO
coupons welcome)

☐ **BILL ME LATER:** (Bill-me option is good on
US/Canada/Mexico orders only; not good to
jobbers, wholesalers, or subscription agencies.)
☐ Check here if billing address is different from
shipping address and attach purchase order and
billing address information.

Signature_____

☐ **PAYMENT ENCLOSED: $**_____

☐ **PLEASE CHARGE TO MY CREDIT CARD.**

☐ Visa ☐ MasterCard ☐ AmEx ☐ Discover
☐ Diner's Club ☐ Eurocard ☐ JCB

Account #_____

Exp. Date_____

Signature_____

Prices in US dollars and subject to change without notice.

NAME_____

INSTITUTION_____

ADDRESS_____

CITY_____

STATE/ZIP_____

COUNTRY_____ COUNTY (NY residents only)_____

TEL_____ FAX_____

E-MAIL_____

May we use your e-mail address for confirmations and other types of information? ☐ Yes ☐ No
We appreciate receiving your e-mail address and fax number. Haworth would like to e-mail or fax special
discount offers to you, as a preferred customer. **We will never share, rent, or exchange your e-mail address
or fax number.** We regard such actions as an invasion of your privacy.

Order From Your Local Bookstore or Directly From
The Haworth Press, Inc.
10 Alice Street, Binghamton, New York 13904-1580 • USA
TELEPHONE: 1-800-HAWORTH (1-800-429-6784) / Outside US/Canada: (607) 722-5857
FAX: 1-800-895-0582 / Outside US/Canada: (607) 771-0012
E-mail to: orders@haworthpress.com

For orders outside US and Canada, you may wish to order through your local
sales representative, distributor, or bookseller.
For information, see http://haworthpress.com/distributors

(Discounts are available for individual orders in US and Canada only, not booksellers/distributors.)

PLEASE PHOTOCOPY THIS FORM FOR YOUR PERSONAL USE.
http://www.HaworthPress.com   BOF04